WHERE LOVE COULD TAKE ME

IRMA SHEPPARD

2014

Copyright © 2014 by Irma Sheppard
All rights reserved

The poems and prose pieces listed below first appeared in the following journals, some in slightly different versions:
July Literary Press: "Best Shot."
Oasis: "Bus Stop," "Silesia: April 1945."
facets: "Not Too Soon."
Our Spirit, Our Reality: "Bus Stop."

Acknowledgements

I thank all those whom I met along the way, for each one has helped me move forward in some particular way I recognize now, but may not have then.

I especially thank my husband, Karl Moeller, for his loving support, patience, skill and enthusiasm in effecting the publication of this book.

In eternal gratitude for the Presence of Meher Baba in my life.

Also by Irma Sheppard

Inheritance

Edited and Co-authored by Irma Sheppard

Beads On One String Tour 2010
Beads-on-One-String Heartland Pilgrimage 2013

CONTENTS

Germany	9
Canada	27
Michigan, USA	99
Venice Beach, California	125
Norfolk, Virginia	171
Tucson, Arizona	185
Village Avenue, Tucson	221

Introduction

I wrote these prose pieces and poems over the years between 2000 and 2014. Sometimes they overlap in telling events in my life, since I wrote them from different perspectives and years apart. With all the gaps and overlaps, this is clearly not an autobiography, yet it is the journey of my life.

--Irma Sheppard
August 2014

GERMANY

First Memory: Silesia, Spring 1945

Standing at the window, I see a stork land on the roof next door. He settles by the nest near the chimney where his mate is sitting on eggs. I am almost one and a half. *Mutti's* sitting at the dressing table, looking in the mirror. Her hair brushed, held back with tortoise shell combs. She glides red lipstick over her upper lip, presses her lips together two, three times.

"Where going?" I ask
"Oh, I have to go see someone."

She doesn't look at me, dabs cologne behind her ears, then between her breasts. I never saw her do that before.

"*Ich auch.* I go too."
"*Nein*, you stay home with Daddy."

Daddy's in his workshop fixing a wheel for someone's wagon. Ilse must be at school. "But I want to." She brushes the shoulders of her best dress, navy with white trim.

"Not today, *Schatzie*." Slides stockinged feet into her good shoes. She doesn't understand how much I need to go with her, don't want to be left home. I walk over to her.

"*Muss mitkommen*. I *have* to." She rarely refuses me anything. I am her *Goldschatz*. If I ask sweet enough, she'll give in. But I won't cry this time. I wrap my arms around her arm and kisskiss the warm skin below her sleeve. She always likes it when I kiss her. Cologne tickles my nose.

"*Nein, Irmchen.*"

"Please. *Bitte, bitteschön.* Pretty please." I give her my sunniest smile. She *can't* resist me now.

But she strokes the top of my head, and gets up.
"You're going to stay with Daddy today." Her voice sounds throaty and thick, not one I've ever heard from her.

"*Nicht* Daddy." My skin prickles. "*Du.*" I twine myself around her leg. She pries me off. I reach for her hand but she gives me a hard look.

Her face is flushed, somehow not the one I know—not just because of the lipstick and powder. Not *my Mutti*. She pulls on her coat, arranges the veil of her little hat over her eyes. I hang on to a chair, speechless with disbelief, watching this *Mutti* step out the door.

Silesia: April, 1945

"*Seh doch nach die Mutter.* Look after Mother," Daddy says to Mutti. He pushes her suitcase under the seat and flings the smaller one into the baggage net overhead. Holding me tight, Mutti sits down by the window, motions for Ilse, six, to sit next to us, and Daddy settles his mother next to her. Across from us, Onkel Willie and his family, all bundled and pinch-faced, are shoving suitcases wherever they may fit. Baskets of *Schnitten, Käse, Äpfel, Kaffee*—sandwiches, cheese, apples, coffee—are tucked between the mothers' feet.

The oily, smoky stink of the train is new in my nostrils. I am one and a half. I sit quiet in Mutti's lap. Quiet, with big eyes. I don't understand all their words, but their tone makes me pay attention to everything they do. Mutti herself is quivering in her softness, her heart beating against my back. I try to curl my toes, but they're too tight inside two pairs of socks. I reach for Mutti's finger instead, and keep hold of it.

"*Wo fahren wir?* Where are we going?" Cousin Leonhardt asks.

"*Ssht,*" his mother tells him. Then softer, "We don't know yet where we'll end up. *Wann sehen wir uns wieder?* When will we see you again?" she asks her husband, and looks to Daddy too.

"*Wiss mir nicht.* Don't know," Daddy says, glancing at his mother. Oma rocks herself, arms crossed against her chest, eyes closed, moaning softly. Daddy crouches, touches her arm. She opens her eyes, reaches out to grasp his hand.

"*Du musst mitkommen.* You have to come with us," she tells him. Separating the families was not the women's choice.

"*Ja Mutter. Aber die Russen kommen, sein bald hier.* The Russians are almost here. You remember how it was in Romania, people disappearing in the night. You have to go now. We'll come soon."

The Russian army less than two days away. Women and children, wearing layers and layers of clothes, are leaving now. I can still see Ilse lugging a suitcase with both hands, trying so hard to keep it off the ground. The men will load tools bedding and kitchenware onto wagons. Hope to meet up. But where?

Oma shakes her head, mutters, *"Kann nicht. Kann es nicht machen.* I can't, I just can't do this." Too ill for the journey.

"Nu," Daddy says, standing up, facing Mutti now. His eyes tell her again to look after his mother. He pats Ilse's blonde pigtails, tells her to help Mutti, then caresses my cheek. Daddy and Onkel Willie back out of the train compartment and my face tightens as if they have taken all the air out with them. We are silent. And still. Even Oma sits quiet. We see them outside the window, now splattered with raindrops. There are no more last words. *Auf wiedersehen* is a prayer in our hearts.

"Alle einsteigen! All aboard!" calls the conductor.

I bump gently back into Mutti's breast, hear the beginning ch-chuh ch-chuh, ch-chuh ch-chuh of my first train ride, and Daddy's face is gone from the window. Sudden hot tears fall on my hand. I twist around. *"Nicht weinen.* Don't cry, Mutti," I say.

But Willie's wife is crying too, and her daughters. Even Ilse sniffles. I can't help it, I join in. Leonhardt, dry-eyed, thumps a suitcase with his scuffed oxfords. Oma is rocking again, beyond tears.

At the next station, Oma says, *"Ich muss weg---Arzt finden.* I have to go find a doctor."

"Nein," Mutti tells her. "The Russian army is still too close."

Next stop, Oma tries to leave the compartment. The women restrain her. Mutti hands me over to Ilse, sits next to Oma, holds her, talks to her still about the Russians, what they do to German women, even the old ones. Three towns later, it's dark outside. We've nodded off to the train's hypnotic rhythm. When it stops, Oma quickly, quietly, lets herself out.

Mutti hears the latch, calls to her, rushes after. But Oma pushes her away and slips into the crowd on the platform. Mutti calls and calls after her.

"Alle einsteigen!"

Mutti shrieking now. Frantic. Clambers back up the steps of the train, looking for the name of this town. The train starts ch-chuh ch-chuh, ch-chuh ch-chuh. Oma lost in the crowd. Gone.

Disbelief of her departure pushes and pulls at our skin. We look at her seat, empty in the corner. Our senses demand she be there, rocking. Shock drains our tears. We cannot sleep. We cannot eat. For a long time we cannot even speak.

A few months later, we are reunited with Daddy in Bavaria. He goes to the Red Cross, tries to find his mother, checks all hospitals and clinics in that vicinity. They find no trace. Despite all our efforts, she has disappeared into the night.

Witzelsdorf, Bavaria: 1947-1948

Early summer, Mom and I and other villagers hang on to wooden side benches as Frau Heilmeier's farm wagon jolts along the dirt road. We're headed for her bean field. Ilse must be in school, and Dad is fixing someone's axle. I do my best with the hoe I'm given, but at four, I'm just old enough to know they wouldn't like to see how many plants I chop into. At lunchtime I abandon the hoe, knowing I am no friend to bean-stalks. Someone cuts thick slices of horseradish, salts and lays them on equally thick slabs of black bread. They pour chicory coffee, *ersatz*, they say. Not the real thing. I am hungry. It is delicious.

Riding on the back of Mom's bicycle, I hold my aching legs out as far as I can so they don't get caught in the spokes. Ilse rides on the bar of Dad's bike. He's put these bikes together from scraps he found around the village, a wheel here, a handlebar there—now our family transportation. We cycle to the woods, spend the day picking blueberries. Mom sings an old folktune to warn me off the fringed toadstools, so pretty—red with white spots. Edible mushrooms Ilse and I pick in the cow pasture behind the farmhouse. Bring apronfuls to Mom, who does her magic—slices, sautés, creams them. We eat them with *mamaliga*—cornmeal mush. We eat everything with *mamaliga*. Maybe because Dad likes it so much, ever since he ate it as a young man in the Romanian army. Maybe because that's just all there is. One day I say to Mom, "Are you making that *mamaliga* again!? Don't you dare cook that again tomorrow!" I am young enough that she still laughs, tells the story to Dad and our landlady, Frau Heilmeier.

Summer, I run barefoot through the grasses by the river, making friends with the buttercups and forget-me-nots—*Vergissmeinnicht*. Pick reeds for Ilse to weave little chairs, tables and beds for make-believe dolls. Nettles grow around the pump in the farmyard. They must like the water that spills over the barrel when we wash our hands, and in the evening our feet, before bedtime. I have to watch out not to brush my bare legs up against them. Once is enough. I don't know how Mom manages to not get stung when she cuts, then rinses them under the pump. She chops them to bits, boils and drains them. Makes a roue, *Einbrenn*, she calls it—brown some flour in butter, add salty cook water, then the nettles, and finally stir in some cream. Imagine—I hear her say— cream, after all these years. *Spinat*, she tells us. It tastes so good. Later, in Canada, she cooks real spinach, and I can't taste the difference. I never understand how Canadian and American kids make such a fuss about hating spinach.

At harvest time I ride with Mom and other workers in the wooden, horse-drawn wagon. They scythe wheat, tie it up in bundles. Weeks earlier when the heavy-headed stalks were already taller than me, I skipped through the sundappled sea of wheat, dotted with flaming poppies—*Mohnblumen*, cornflowers and daisies—*Margaretenblumen*. But now the field lies in rows of stubble, which pricks my bare feet. I find no place even to sit. I don't know what to do with myself. Hot and itchy, I cry. I bawl. Exasperated, Mom lifts me up and deposits me in a patch of friendly green, where Queen Anne's lace, chicory and caraway scent the air. Content, I pick caraway seeds and chew them. Early fall, I dig for potatoes in the innkeeper's field, alongside Mom, Dad, Ilse and other villagers. Three bags of potatoes for our labors. Haying season and I ride home, high on top of the towering, swaying, sweet-smelling hay.

The men of the village cut blocks of ice from the river in winter. The kids are all warned to stay away—could be dangerous, someone falling into open water. Dad is smart in ways of how to do things, tells the men where to cut first—he's in charge, even though he's just a refugee, living in Frau H.'s front room. Ilse has figured out that with Dad's standing among the villagers, she can do what other kids aren't allowed. So she takes me down to watch them stack huge blocks of ice on a big sled, sprinkle them with sawdust to store in the innkeeper's icehouse. Cool through the summer. Afterward, the men regale each other over *Bier* at the inn, rehash the day's work. Bottles of red cream soda appear for Ilse and me, the first I've ever tasted.

Spring, and I plant calendula with Frau Heilmeier, in flowerbeds behind the farmhouse. I help pack moist loam over the seeds. Maybe Dad talks her into planting onions, garlic and lettuce too for the table. A few years later, in Canada, he talks our Hungarian landlord into letting him dig up three-quarters of our back yard for a vegetable garden. Still later, as he builds a house for us, he and Mom put in a garden covering most of the backyard. Tomatoes, onions, garlic, beans, lettuce, dill, parsley, corn, cucumbers, beets, parsnips, cabbages, potatoes, kohlrabi, strawberries, huckleberries, peach trees, and flowers—snapdragons, gladioli, asters, marigolds for Mom. Finally in Michigan, outside Detroit, another garden, this time with raspberry canes, pear trees and cherries too. I can't help but wonder why Frau Heilmeier planted a whole bed of golden orange calendula in post-war Germany.

What I Knew

Nein, she said, when my father asked for a room
in her farmhouse—the children would be a bother.
He swore not. Pointed out his wife'd help with harvests,
that she could bake—*Brot und Torten*. He'd make currying
brushes from horsetails, barrels for sauerkraut, build
a new outhouse—what she, a middle-aged spinster
with a half-wit brother could not. We moved into her parlor.
By spring I followed her like a pet, from the brood hen
under her stove to the henhouse for eggs. Pestered and charmed
her with my three-year-old's questions and musings.

Nein, he said, when she asked to adopt me, promising
the farm would be mine after her. I'd marry well.
A grand offer to refugees who'd lost everything in the war.

Nein, I said, when she took to asking me to spend a night
with her. But I did want to please her. One day I said *ja*,
and in my nightie bravely marched down the hall that evening,
up stairs I'd never climbed before, and into her room.

A big bed, high with feather comforter.
Air close and damp, a hint of henhouse.
Her hair down in one long plait.
Something inside me stopped
but my body climbed into the bed.
Like a hand over my mouth,
the quilt closed over me

Nein, nein, nein, I screamed.

Explosion of arms, legs.
A wail surrounded me,
tumbled me down the stairs, down the hall.
Mutti! Mutti!
Not knowing what it was that I knew.

Differences

As a child of three and four in a Bavarian village after WWII, the parameters of my daily life consisted of the room we lived in, the farmyard and its outbuildings, the cow pasture, the crop fields, the woods and occasional visits to an aunt, the inn, the river. Mainly the farmyard, chasing pigeons and piglets.

When I was four we began the process of emigrating to Canada, which entailed several train trips to various emigration camps. We were having a meal in the dining car and the waiter came to attend to us. Eyes wide, I blurted out, "*Aber Mutti, er ist schwarz!*" But Mummy, he is black!

She probably shushed me up with a look, but I suspect she had never seen a Black person before either. I had never even heard of such a person. I don't remember how the waiter responded to my outburst--I imagine I continued to examine him in wonder and perplexity--so he must have had the grace to simply take our order.

From the Train

A girl my age, four or five, stood in her backyard, watching the train go by. Arms raised, hands clasped behind her head. I see her through the years as I saw her in that moment, as I sat on the train clattering north to Hanover, to the ship that carried me across the Atlantic. As I sat seeing this girl my age in a white blouse, a dark skirt, her hair brown like mine but longer, watching my train pass her by, I thought how her life would be different from mine. She in her backyard staying and I on the train leaving this shattered country. I knew in a flash I would never forget her, would return to the image of her arms raised, hands clasped behind her head, and wonder what her life would be. I had no sense, no picture of what I was hurtling toward.

Moving On

A pyramid of small oranges each wrapped in a square of tissue, dessert in the macaroni and cheese lunch line. I hold my very first orange, watch others peel off the thin skins, and do the same. Bitter oils squirt my eyes and nose, sting my fingers, and the pretty orange fruit----sour, miserably sour….

    …next day I try to trade off the daily orange--no takers.

I think of the dark red Christmas apples from our village in Bavaria, snow white and sweet inside. How we cycled to the woods, Ilse and me riding double with Daddy and Mutti, to pick luscious blueberries all day. Mushrooms, earthy from the cow pasture behind the farm house—sliced and creamed….

    …spooned over slabs of *mamaliga*—cornmeal mush.

And the sweet green smell of buttercups, yellow dots in a field of clover. Golden wheat fields laced with poppies, cornflowers, daisies. Me straddling fragrant hay as the wagon trundled to the barn. Chasing farmyard pigeons, cuddling rabbit babies ….

...but now this rolling deck of the Beaversbrae

douses me with nausea every other day as it plows through the Atlantic from Bremershafen to Quebec City. "Good-night Irene" the first song I hear in English--I don't understand a word. My fifth birthday on the ship—no presents. A boy tries to push me down a shaft open to the sea. A girl my age tells me each morning that today the ship will definitely sink…

...and every day a pyramid of bitter oranges awaits me.

Turning Five

Birthdays came out of the blue, as on my fourth when Ilse, gripping a small bunch of *Vergissmeinnicht,* walked me backward into a corner. I felt a little nervous. I never knew with my older sister—all those recurring dreams. But she stuck her arm out offering me the flowers and recited a little verse. I didn't know what was going on until, grinning, she wished me a happy birthday, all pleased now with her snappy delivery.

Refugees, we paused in a Bavarian village for three years after the war. Dad talked Frau Heilmeier into letting us stay, the four of us in her former parlor, telling her all the things he could fix on her farm. He was a wheelwright, a wagonmaker, could make almost anything, made two bicycles for family transportation from after-the-war scraps. Our room had a wood cookstove, a galvanized bucket for water from the farmyard pump, cots, a table and chairs. Fleeing the Russians, spring of '45, we hadn't brought much from Silesia—tools, kitchen things, clothes we outgrew.

I'd skip through a field of ripening wheat, the stalks taller than me, daisies, poppies, cornflowers waving in the dappled light. I'd chase pigeons into the outhouse, ride atop the swaying haywagon, smell the sharp yellow of buttercups, run terrified from the top-hatted, black-faced chimneysweeps on their black bicycles, and stay clear of the gypsy caravans on the road, because they were sure to steal me. Fed piglets with baby bottles, collected eggs, gathered mushrooms from the cow pasture out back, and picked blueberries in the woods.

But in spring and summer of '48 we rode train after train, ate canned chicken (sent by Dad's sisters from New York) between slices of *Mutti's* dark *Rogenbrot*, shuttling from one emigration camp to another for several months because *Mutti* tested positive for TB. We stood in lines with aluminum bowls for soup, stood almost naked in more lines in Quonset huts, to show teeth, stick out tongues, to breathe deeply for the doctors and their icy stethoscopes. Turned out we were flat-footed, the whole family. Ilse went off to English classes, taught us how to say, "yes, no, please, thank you, hello, good-bye." Dad played his pearly, red-buttoned accordian one last time in a hollow by the road, then sold it. *Mutti* cried a lot.

Embarked on the Beaverbrae in *Bremerhaven*—mid-October, maybe the eighteenth, 1948. Women and small children in cavernous dorms with four-bed bunks. Me alone in a top bunk, sleepless and tossing that first night listening to "Goodnight

Irene" on the watchman's radio. How did I know it was "Goodnight Irene?" Dad was quartered with the men elsewhere on the ship. We visited him sometimes because, nauseous and sick the whole journey, he rarely got out of bed. Mutti and Ilse lay abed often, not well either, so I was mostly on my own, hanging out with a girl my age, exploring the decks, the dining halls, the stairways. This girl assured me daily, on the good authority of her mother, that our ship was reallyreally going to sink today. However, the Beaverbrae ploughed on west through the rough Atlantic. Flying fish accompanied us in small teams as we hung with excitement, cold and a little nausea onto the railing. From time to time crewmen laughingly tossed candy and chocolate bars into scrabbling clots of children. I caught only the hot, but boring white peppermints.

You'd think that daily oranges would have been an exotic delight to us all, refugees who'd survived on uncertain and curtailed food supplies for the past several years. Each time we slid our trays with bowls of soup, flimsy white bread and pats of salted butter down the counter, a pyramid of oranges sat at the end, each orange wrapped in a square of green tissue. I'd never seen a orange before. We took the first ones gladly, but found them uniformly sour. Then we would take one—it was food— thinking perhaps it would taste sweeter later. Tried to pass them off. We even tried the crew—an orange for a chocolate bar? Hah. Sometimes they'd give us a peppermint, but they never took the derelict oranges.

A few days into the Atlantic, *Mutti* said it was my fifth birthday, and Ilse added, "So you're five years old today." That struck me as a true wonder—my birthday and on the very same day, I was five years old. Imagine! This extended my counting ability by one. Up to now I'd counted only to four: *eins, zwei, drei, vier*. Now I had *fünf* to boot. Life was magnificent.

That same day, a bully boy pushed me over the edge of a shaft on the deck, at the bottom of which I saw the grey Atlantic churning. Dad was watching from his upper deck railing, and he always told the story afterward, proud of me, as if I'd done something truly great. I'd been peering down, fascinated by the roiling waters, suddenly a shove, and I was over the shaft. Without thinking I stretched my legs far as I could, gained foothold on the other side and watched the boy scuttle fast away. I have always wondered, what was he thinking? I could have fallen into the ocean. Drowned. On my fifth birthday.

On October 28th, we landed in Quebec City, Canada. We disembarked with suitcases and a wooden trunk Dad had made, filled with feather pillows, down quilts, woolens, tools and *Mutti's* treasured red leather boots. No toys. Only essentials to help us survive Canadian winters. We boarded a National Pacific train and chugged west for three days. Wearing my best dress of wine red pleated gabardine with a white linen collar, I slept cozy in the baggage net above the seats, a perfect hammock for a squirmy five-year-old.

Saskatchewan. Regina. Snow higher than my head. *Mutti's* brother, Onkel John, met us at the station. She introduced us and we piled into his pickup.

"Irmhild!" he bellowed. "Canadians will break their tongues on that. You have to change your name."

CANADA

Immigrant Experience

We arrived in Regina, Saskatchewan after a three-day train trip from Quebec City. We had with us the trunk my father made, filled with feather pillows and quilts to keep us warm in Canadian winters. We had spent many hours stripping the feathers of their stems, so Mom could sew them into new bedding. I was sad there'd been no room for the lovely dolls and cradles and other toys my parents had made for our last Christmas in Germany. But our Canadian relatives presented Ilse and me with new and fancier dolls for our first Christmas in Canada.

As far as I was aware, I lacked for nothing. Despite the war and its aftermath, I had never gone hungry or unsheltered. Thanks to our relatives in New York, we'd received boxes of hand-me-down coats, sweaters and shoes, with Hershey chocolate bars and Christmas gifts tucked in between.

During the long prairie winter of 1948-1949 I stayed with my parents on my uncle's farm, while Ilse stayed in town with his family so she could go to school and learn English. On sunny days the two farm dogs helped me explore wind-swept snowdrifts around the farm buildings. Otherwise the land was flat and white as far as I could see in any direction. On blizzard or snowy days, I whiled away the hours exploring whatever my Canadian cousins had left behind in their closets and cupboards—broken toys, scribbled up coloring books, broken crayons, school readers. And old Simpson-Sears catalogs.

My life on the little Bavarian farm had been rich with running barefoot in grassy fields, picking poppies, cornflowers and buttercups. Ilse and I picked mushrooms in the cow pasture. I followed our landlady as she collected eggs every morning. I entertained her with my acute observations in her kitchen, wary all the while of the testy brood hen setting under the stove. We swam in the river, dug for potatoes alongside the villagers, watched as the men cut the river ice for the innkeeper's cellar. Life was good from my three- and four-year-old perspective. Life was full and lacked for nothing.

On Uncle John's farm, old coloring books, readers and catalogs opened Pandora's Box. I awakened to a world of wanting. I wanted my own coloring book, new, so I could color Tinker Bell and Cinderella instead of Porky Pig or Goofy, who'd already been scribbled over. From the pictures in the reader I saw goblets of ice cream and sparkling red Jello and stacks of bananas and pineapples, none of which I'd ever seen in my life. Dick and Jane and Spot entered my life prematurely. I couldn't read, of course, but in later years I put names to all these images that I pored over and burned into awareness.

The Simpson-Sears catalog was a world in itself. Little girls with ponytails in frilly pink dresses. Children riding tricycles, tossing blue and white balls. Girls jumping with skip ropes. None of which I'd ever seen. I wanted a pair of snow boots with furry lining spilling over the tops. I wanted a coat with its hood trimmed in white fur. I wanted the shiny black shoes with straps below the ankles. Page after page showed me a world, a life not mine. The pain of not having arose and grew. In this new country, I was a little girl who did not have.

The Telephone Call - 1948

I was five that first winter, when we lived on Uncle John's farm outside Regina, Saskatchewan. Although we'd lived on a farm in Bavaria after the war, there were many things new to me on this farm. Here there were below freezing temperatures and snow higher than my head. There were two dogs to play with and a horse to pull a sled. There was a flush toilet in the cellar. And in the hallway there was a telephone, the first I'd ever seen.

The telephone was mounted on the wall, with the speaking horn protruding from its wooden case. The cylindrical earpiece hung from a cord and was placed against one's ear. They let me listen once to Uncle John's hearty "Hello, hello," but I was too little to reach the speaker horn, and too young to have anything important to say.

On the occasions when it rang, the number of rings indicated if the call was for us. If she was home for the weekend, my sister would answer, speak with the operator to get connected with the caller. Ilse was the only one in our family who was learning English at that time. When a call wasn't for us, we looked at the telephone with curiosity and apprehension.

I dreamed one night that an elderly relative in Regina had died. In the morning, before breakfast, the telephone rang our set of rings. My father picked up the earpiece. With virtually no English he managed to understand the operator and respond appropriately to accept Uncle John's call. Mom and I stood watching his face as he listened and made a few short comments.

He hung the earpiece up on its rung, and turned to us. The elderly woman I'd dreamt of, he told us, had died in the night.

I enjoyed the small fuss my parents made over my precognitive dream. What I couldn't convey to them was that this coincidental event awakened me to a deeper part of myself. I became aware of a new level of knowing within myself. In Germany I'd already had dreams which came to guide me, and which I came to trust.

Everything Is New

I am five years old, walking to Victoria School,
My sister leads the way.
It's a drizzly morning early in April, 1949 in Windsor.
Everything is new: bananas, ice cream, kindergarten.

We make our first turn at a stately funeral home,
fronted by yards of lush lawn.
Young blades of grass glow neon green despite cloudy skies,
raindrops magnify their exuberant zest.

Spring flowers grace the corner of the lawn.
I stop, enchanted.
Blazing riot of reds, yellows, purples. And the green.
I stand entranced.

Sister pokes my arm,
reminds me she's still there,
says in German, *C'mon, we have to go!*
I follow her, dragging my heels.

Part of me stands on that corner still.

The Window

Yellow tulips, and red, with green stems and leaves, cut from thick paper, taped high onto the bay window. The teacher cut them, each one perfectly. I stand close to the low oak sill. Noiseless rain shrouds the playground. A bright green apron of grass spreads out to the walk. Lilac clusters jigjig under the April raindrops. It's early morning, class not yet started. Behind me children shout and chatter. Clink-thud of toys and games. Snip-swoosh of scissors and paper. I take in the excited hubbub of their voices, but I don't understand the words. I stand alone watching the rain. Here, nothing expected of me. No trying to make out their words, their meaning. A girl may look at me, but play with someone else—my lack of English keeps everyone away. Even the teacher. Bewildered, she doesn't know what to do with me. The bay window feels safe, the rain familiar. I am five years old, dropped last week into this kindergarten. I need to go to the bathroom, move closer to the teacher's desk. Put the words together. Keep them silent in the shyness of my tongue. She is busy. No moment alone, so I can whisper my need. Keep my eyes steadfast on her, hope she will see me. But the language barrier keeps me invisible. The bell rings. We go to our seats. I gaze longingly at the familiar rain, the sheltering window. I know how to say it. I heard other kids ask.

My First Friend

Sherry Morgan was my first friend in Canada, in fact, my first friend at all. We were in first grade together at Prince Edward elementary school. She lived across the street from me with her mother, grandmother and little brother. Her mom was tall, a handsome woman, with hair and skin much darker than Sherry's. Her brother had a mass of dark curly hair, very different from Sherry's light brown, slightly kinked hair. Did I know not to ask, where's your Daddy?

Granma I remember sitting quietly watchful in the kitchen. I was allowed to visit and welcome to come back, Granma said, because I was polite and respectful. I didn't know any other way to be. In the village back in Bavaria, when I met anyone, whether I knew them or not, I was to curtsey and say *"Grüss Gott."* Maybe I curtsied to Granma.

Sherry and I walked to school together. She often had toffee or cherry lifesavers, and after the second or third time she also had an elaborate explanation about why she wasn't allowed to share them with me.

Whatever English I knew by that September, I'd learned in a few months of kindergarten and playing with kids since April. I learned a lot from Sherry—all about number one and number two, for example, in case I needed to explain it to the teacher, who was also Miss Morgan, but white. And what to call the strange sensations in my belly on the way to school every morning: "You have a stomach egg," Sherry informed me. I had that stomach egg for years, before it dawned on me it was a stomach ache. And many years more before I realized that stomach ache was really about needing to take time to do a number two.

After school, Sherry would grab me and urgently tell me that Joe Morgan, from theclan on Mercer Street behind us, (distant cousins, she said) was going to beat us up. No particular reason. Just because. Joe was a couple of years older and seemed a likely threat. So we'd find an unexpected door to sneak out of, and alleys to run through until she declared us safe again for the day.

It never occurred to me that I never heard Joe threaten us, that he never chased us. I just remember seeing him lounging on the school steps once. He said something to me, made a suggestion I didn't understand, except that by the expression on his face I knew it was not nice, but something he thought he would enjoy. Was this what he'd said to her?

Before the end of first grade we moved a few blocks closer to the school. I got to know the kids on that street—all white. I spent most of second grade on Long Island, staying with relatives. By third grade I was back in Windsor, and Sherry and I were in the same class again, but we didn't play much together any more. I don't know why.

Walking Home

>skipping on sidewalks
>>slippery with silvery
>>>wet red maple leaves

Highland Avenue

Our neighbors on Highland Avenue in Windsor were an older couple with an adopted teenage daughter. This girl was strange in almost every way. Her face looked like it had been burned, scar tissue veins criss-crossing angry red skin. Her hair hung in dark braids down her back. She wore loose, flowered cotton dresses. Her speech was garbled, with turkey-like tones. She seemed angry and threatening, sitting on their veranda as we played in the street.

The neighborhood kids told me she was Indian. I was five and my English very limited, so I had no idea what that meant. Some of the boys yelled at her, called her names. She'd stomp down the steps, storm in her eyes, ranting in her turkey-talk, waving her arms. They said she was crazy. From her appearance and behavior I began to have an inkling of what that meant. We'd scatter as someone came from inside the house to calm her down and take her in.

I was scared of her, but also was aware of the kids' meanness toward her. One night I had a startling dream about her. I was in a car, locking all the doors, raising the windows because she was trying to get in. When I looked out again, I saw her head on the street, talking to me, warning me. I was terrified.

From this dream I understood I was never to make fun of such a person. Taboo to taunt them, make fun of or speak ill of them. While I had no language for any of this, I understood I had always to keep a real respect for each person, no matter what they looked or sounded like, no matter how they behaved.

First Thanksgiving: Windsor, 1949

Bring something
for our cornucopia,
Miss Morgan says.

I choose a silken yellow pear
for the curvy horn set up
in our first grade classroom.

Recent images of grinning pumpkins
still glow in my mind—
I chisel a happy face into my golden pear.

Proudly present it to Miss Morgan,
who frowns and not unkindly, says,
But you're not supposed to nibble on it.

I see the pear in her hand,
see the cuts I made last night
now curling in on themselves,
shrivelled, turning brown.

Too hard to explain
in my beginning English—
my glorious pear
brought so low.

My Sixth Birthday

By October 1949, we had lived in Windsor for six months, and Mom was seeing distinct advantages of living in a Canadian city rather than in a post-war Bavarian village. In addition to having an indoor toilet, hot and cold running water in the house, shopping just blocks away, she could also attend to what she must have seen as a cruel trick of nature—not only was I not a *Goldkopf* like my sister, but my brown hair was straight, just like my father's.

She marched me to the end of our block, where she had noted a small beauty shop. Ilse came too because she was the only one of us who could speak English. They left me there with the very nice hairdresser.

All morning—hours of shampoo, haircut, smelly perm solutions dripping and burning my scalp and neck, hot hair dryers. Mom and Ilse came to collect me just as the curlers came out and presto—nothing! My hair was straight as ever.

Mom was not pleased, and it wasn't just about the ten dollars she'd wheedled out of Dad. How we looked reflected on her. She could count on Ilse to outclass cousin Erna's three daughters, none of whom were blonde or curly. But me—how did she get saddled with a *Strumplpeter* like me!

The nice hairdresser apologized—the perm didn't take—but she'd do it over again. My eyes grew large with horror. But there was no question of asking what I wanted. Again many smelly, drippy, burning hot hours. Again—nothing. I skipped all the way home in the fresh cool air. I didn't care about my hair. I think that perm was supposed to be my birthday present. All afternoon Mom had put together a birthday feast, invited Erna and her family, expecting her very own version of Shirley Temple to be seated in the place of honor.

Years later, during my teens and twenties, Mom would say to me from time to time, "Irma, wouldn't you like to have a nice little perm?" And I would roll my eyes.

Letter Not Sent

Dear Jackie Penny, October 22, 1949

    I like the way you run around a lot. And the way your hair sticks up blond in front. I wish you were my boyfriend instead of Maureen's. I can see why you always pick her for the Bluebird dance—she's so pretty with curls and dimples and cute dresses. I wish you would pick me sometime, even if I am a lot taller than you. I've seen you kiss her cheek. I'm new here in Prince Edward's first grade. I'm new in Windsor. I'm new in Canada. Just now learning English. I wish someone were sweet to me. Mummy and Daddy are always so busy, working and worrying, and Ilse mostly bosses me around. I feel sad and mad when I see you and Maureen with your heads together. I wish you were my boyfriend, Jackie Penny, even if you are kind of short. Your name is so cute.

    Your secret girlfriend,
    Irma

A Delicate Moment

My parents spoke only *Hochdeutsch*, High German, to my sister and me when we lived in Germany. My mother said that when she married my father and moved to the larger town he was from, she was mortified because they spoke *Hochdeutsch*, and she knew only their common dialect. She swore that her children would never experience that embarrassment.

After we'd come to Canada, she and my father reverted to their everyday dialect when they spoke to each other, which, at first I didn't understand. I remember asking my sister one time, "What did *Mutti* say?"

My father claimed to speak six languages. He and *Mutti* grew up in what is now Romania, where over the centuries many cultures and languages cohabited, so he was conversant in German, Ukrainian, Romanian, Hungarian, Yiddish and finally, English. My mother also spoke Ukrainian and Romanian. When they didn't want us to understand what they were saying, they spoke in Ukrainian.

After a couple of years in Windsor, Canada, my parents still spoke to me in *Hochdeutsch* and I answered in English. My mother used to say to visitors, referring to me, "She understands everything (in German), but she won't speak a word."

Perhaps out of delicacy and consideration for our tender ears, when my father swore, he swore in Ukrainian or Romanian. He did this often enough that the phrases stuck in my head. To this day I am multilingual in my capacity to swear. I am thankful that I have lost virtually all interest in doing so.

We used to have boarders in our home to augment our income--Germans, Ukrainians, a Romanian, a Greek. When I was eight, our boarder was Romanian, an arrogant man, full of himself. I didn't like him much. One evening I was sprawled as usual on the living room floor reading the funnies as my mother cooked dinner in the kitchen. The boarder entered the front door and stood there expectantly. I ignored him, busy with "Nancy and Sluggo."

"Hey! You're supposed to get up and say hello to me when I come in," he announced in German.

I didn't think so. What popped out of my mouth was one of my father's Romanian oaths. *"Nasera matra."* I can't vouch for the spelling or how many words that consists of, and have now only a vague idea of what improper act it commanded regarding his mother.

"What! You say that to me!"

He marched into the kitchen and repeated it all to my mother. She called me and asked if I'd said that. In this delicate moment I was alert to two things: Mom could easily be violent with me, and Mom didn't much care for this fellow either.

"He said it first," I told her. This was true, though he hadn't said it on this particular occasion.

I didn't look at him. My fate rested with her. She put the wooden spoon down on the counter (a good sign), looked at Mr. Romanian-Full-of-Himself-Man right in the eye and said in her most no-nonsense tone, "Well, it's just like when a cuckoo calls out in the woods--he gets an echo right back."

It sounded better in German, of course, since it was a well-known adage, not anything Mom had to dig for.

That was the end of that--except I never forgot it--one of the very few times she actually took my side. Maybe she was standing up for herself in a way. Years later I learned that she'd been violated at fifteen by her brother-in-law, a Romanian police officer.

The gift of languages was passed on to me. I studied French for eight years, then taught it in high school. I studied Latin for four years, then German, and taught that to adults. Some college Spanish classes. Smatterings of Italian, Latvian, Arabic. Now I'm reviewing my CD lessons in Persian. God willing, I will have an Iranian son-in-law soon. I imagine we will have many opportunities to expand our respective language skills--his English and my Farsi.

Bus Stop

It was already dark that evening, though it was early. It must have been spring or maybe fall, Mom and me standing at the bus stop, wrapped tight against the breezy chill. We stood close that evening, her arm around my shoulder, waiting for the bus.

A thought, maybe a question, flew into my head and with it a small unease that needed to stir. I slipped loose, and with one hand grasping the bus stop post, whirled around onetwothree times, my other hand flying free. Remembering times she'd teased me about my bellybutton or my lisp, little things like that, I thought I'd found a little thing to tease her about.

"You told Aunt Erna you couldn't see her because you were sick."

Her eyes tightened up just a bit in the corners and she said, "Oh that— neveryoumind." I ignored the light warning in her voice. I was six, the darling of my mother's day, the *Goldschatz* of her life. Too young to be taken seriously, I could say whatever came to mind and receive her indulgent smile. I'd always been such a good girl. And she always wanted me to tell her the truth.

"But Mommy, it wasn't true. That was a lie. You lied." I was thinking about Sherry, my best friend in first grade—Sherry with her cinnamon hair in pigtails, her cinnamon skin warm and smooth, and her cinnamon voice, spicy with mock accusations as we teased each other: You lied. No, *you* lied.

Her eyes hardened on me. "Irma, don't be a bad girl!"

"But you *did*."

And then a strange thing.

She came at me, hands opening from fists in her pockets. Eyes narrowed. Fury tearing a hole in her face. I backed up as if stung, put the bus stop post between us. A hollow hammering flared inside my head and down to my stomach. Barely breathing, I peered up at her shadowed face under the yellow light of the street lamp. The night air thickened, smelled for an instant of broken fruit, then furred with static. I'd seen her like this a few times with my older sister. Never with me.

I shut up. For years. Never again teased her. The playful part of me kept the bus stop post forever between us. And she—she leaned on the looming shadow part of herself more and more, hands slapping, wooden spoons beating, voice thundering doom whenever she thought I'd gotten too spunky.

The bus finally came, squealed to a stop. The doors whooshed open and I followed her up the steps, waited as she dropped a nickel and a dime into the fare box. I sat next to her because I knew I had to, careful that the nub of my coat didn't touch hers.

A Five-Christmas Retrospect

We waved hello and goodbye to Mom as she blew kisses down from a third floor window of the Sanatorium. She with TB. Again. On a frosty morning Pastor Friedrichson and his wife put Ilse, twelve, and me, seven, on the train—thirteen hours from Windsor, Canada to Grand Central Station. Aunt Pauline and her family picked us up in their new, sky-blue 1950 Pontiac sedan. June, ten, oohed at the gigantic Christmas tree—blazing clear up into the sky—on the way to Long Island.

Aunt Pauline settled us in with June upstairs, the big room with dormers. June buzzing about Christmas coming, about Santa Claus coming about all the goodies coming, coming. Pictures of Santa Claus drinking Coca Cola, Gene Autry singing "Rudolph the Red-nosed Reindeer," fat bulbs of red, green, blue and yellow lights strung around the front door, sneaking Christmas candy from the dish on the coffee table. "The Lone Ranger" on the ten-inch television Thursday evenings.

June, Ilse and I each received a red, imitation alligator cosmetic case, our names embossed in gold under the latch. Inside, a mirror on the lid. It had the immediate aura of a most prized possession. I used it as a base for my artistic installations to showcase other treasures. We used them as overnight cases on visits to Uncle Martin in Hartsdale, Aunt Katie in White Plains. They bought us presents, gave us quarters. They were all very good to us, but in some way it was like setting cut flowers into rich soil.

In the schoolyard and in the neighborhood, we played as equals (we were "the neighbors from the north"), tuned into and tried out the Long Island accent. But at home there was no getting around the fact (inside my head) that we were the poor cousins whose mother had TB. And toothed memories of the truant officer who'd found us playing hooky and smoking Players cigarettes while Dad was at work. Things Ilse, desperate, bent on being reckless, out of control, had gotten me to do with her.

Christmas at six—Windsor—a lit up tree and me lying in bed alone, feverish with chicken pox. In store windows—candles shaped as evergreen firs, as snowmen, as carolers, with top hats and mufflers. Seven-Up peppering my nose. Presents?

Christmas at five in Regina, Saskatchewan, with *Mutti's* brother and his family. Dolls for Ilse and me, a grocer's wooden fruit basket made do as a cradle. The musty, oily smell of wax fruit in a bowl. The bitter-sour taste of olives I'd taken to be green and red candies on the dinner table. My first taste of ice cream—vanilla.

Weihnachten at four was in Witzelsdorf, Bavaria—candles on the tree, cradles *Vati* made, bedding sewn by *Mutti*, dolls sent by our New York relatives—for Ilse and me. All left behind when we emigrated to Canada the following year.

I remember being told at four that I'd been so excited about *Weihnachten*, about *Sant Niklaus*, the year before at three, that I'd made myself ill. Only a startling memory of small wine-red apples, crisp and white as snow inside.

That Day

My hand homed right in on it—this India rubber ball,
white paint all worn off, now a smooth dusky black.
Found it in the weeds of the empty corner lot where
we played softball. It bounced through the gamut
of *one two three O'Leary* without a miss. Hard and solid,
it sailed back into my palm tight as a boomerang.

> Sitting around that day
> on the wooden rails of June's back porch—
> June and me, my big sister, Ilse,
> and a couple of other kids. I say
> "June and me" as if we were friends—
> we were just neighbors.

Saw her play this game once. Stood
at homeplate facing the red bricks of our rowhouse.
Dared myself to toss my prized ball
over my shoulder, far and high.

Found it straight off in the rut between second
base and third. Hugged it with both hands.
Tossed again with a whopping swoop and turned.
Half my insides sank to my knees. Scuffed the weeds
around first base. Palm aching for my beloved, silky ball.
Dummy, Stoopid.

> Dad told me I did it,
> years later when I was grown up.
> I didn't believe him, but

    Ilse said it was true.

    I was seven then,
    two years younger than anybody.
    June lit into me again that day,
    twitting me about something—
    the color of my shorts, my hair,
    my lisp, my tatty running shoes.
    What she *always* did.
Found it in a clump of timothy just past
second. Gladgladglad. World was right again.
Just one more time. Threw it straight over my head,
hard. Shuddered at the soft thuds. Ran right
to the outfield. Pushed weeds aside with my sneakers.
Over every patch and clump. For hours.

    They say I jumped off the rail,
    popped her in the mouth with my fist.
    Loosened two front teeth. Blood
    dripping on her cotton flowered dress.
    Her mother in the kitchen behind me
    heard it all, didn't say a word to me.

Better Than Church

Sunday before nine, we leave Saturday's sins swept
beneath our beds, pile into Dad's '51 Ford pickup—
Mom, Dad, Doris and Eric, Ilse and me, Jack, our boarder.
Dad heads north, out of Windsor to Belle River.

I am seven and Belle River is my idea of heaven.
Sitting on benches padded with beach blankets,
we sing haunting hymns on the road—*Red River Valley,
Edelweiss, The Tennessee Waltz*—Mom joining in

in German from inside the cab. We tell jokes, laugh
at the warm wind. Stop at a roadside stand for baskets
of cherries, peaches, plums, a watermelon—
Essex County, the Sun Parlour of Canada.

Better than church—the Sunday God smiling upon us.

Finally in the parking lot Dad turns off the ignition—
I slip a black inner tube over my head, jump out,
escape as the others sort their stuff—race to the sandy
beach, itching to splash into the divinely cool water.

I glide and twist, roll and loop for hours in the shallows.
I am reborn. Easter trumpets in my heart, but
my stomach lets me know lunchtime. I find them all
playing Eucher or Sixty-six under the maples and poplars,

trumping each other with shouts and hoots, pushing
pennies, nickels, dimes in small time wins and losses.

"I'm hungry," I tell Mom. "Okay," she says. "After this hand,"
But Dad's on a roll—three, four more rounds. Blessed

by hunger, we stuff ourselves: breaded fried chicken,
potato salad, Mom's pickles, tomatoes from our garden.
Then the cherries, the plums. Eric aims a pit at Doris—
she gets him back, so we swirl in a two minute free-for-all.

Too full, water-washed, sun-rinsed, I loll
on a shaded blanket and doze. Ilse,
under a striped towel and behind a paperback,
evades for now Dad's furtive eye. The sun leans

into the afternoon. She nudges me up—
we collect pop bottles for two-cent deposits,
buy Cokes, chips or Frostbites at the pavillion.
Watch teenage girls, the straps to their bathing
 suits dangling, slowdance to Teresa Brewer
wailing *Baby, Baby, Baby* on the jukebox.
Boys at the pinball machines, shuffle and shout
to their own muscled rat-a-tat, bam-kabam tunes.

Back into the lake, I paddle to the raft—dive, crash
into the water in frenzied denial of Mom's Monday
face. Too soon the glassy water lies empty of the sun's
buttery light. I return, towel off. We reload the truck

in sifting dusk. Sunburned, drowsy, I half hear the
grownups' subdued stories—dreams foam up, fizz out.
Home after dark, I shed my bathing suit still gritty
with sand, and surrender to the mystery of sleep.

Standing in the Corner

"Irma stood in the corner again today." Ilse telling Mom. Why? Hoping I'd get smacked like she did when she'd been corrected by the nuns in Bavaria.

But it was true, in third grade I stood in the corner a lot. Miss McKinley must have been in her sixties or more. Short curly grey hair, kind of plump. Face like a potato gone too soft, heart like a walnut. She didn't have a clue about eight-year-olds. It was 1951 in Windsor, so in retrospect, I wouldn't expect enlightened classroom attitudes. In first grade, Mr. Gibson the hefty principal, whumped my behind because I was talking as we lined up in squadrons, ready to march through the wide doors of Prince Edward elementary school. That same year the speech teacher (I used to lisp) sat me in front, tripped over my already long legs and sent me to Mr. Gibson's office. He obliged by strapping my palms. It didn't hurt so much. I just didn't understand.

Like I didn't understand being sent to the corner so often.

It would go like this. Miss McKinley'd give us some work to do, maybe so many pages of multipication. I'd do it. I'd check my work. I'd read my favorite stories in the Reader (for the umpteenth time): Aladdin and the Magic Lamp, The Tin Soldier, Sinbad the Sailor. I'd linger over the pictures, put myself into the stories. Recheck my arithmetic. Fiddle with my pencil, bite it to make a pattern in the yellow paint, chew on its eraser, drop it, bend down to pick it up....but Manfred, behind me, had his foot on it.

"Move your foot."

He'd grin, slung low over his desk so she couldn't see.

"Let me get my pencil." I'd grab for it and....

"Irma! What are you doing? Go to the corner. Now."

Manfred still grinning, sideways now at Herbert. The dweebs. No sense of German immigrant kids sticking together. They drew endless pictures of bombers and fighter planes, show them to each other slyly. They never got sent to the corner. That was part of what I didn't understand. Or how come it always took the other kids so long to do the arithmetic problems.

I know now that I was a squirmy kid and I'd run out of things to do with myself. Shouldn't the teacher have figured out that I needed extra projects or a good book to read? Being social like my father, I'd turn to my neighbors, see if they were done, or what. But it seemed always to come down to...

"Irma! Go stand in the corner."

And there I'd be when the bell rang for the upper grades to change classes, and Ilse got to peek in—see me standing there.

"Irma, do you stand in the corner every day?" Mom asked one day after Ilse's punctual report.

"No, Mom," I sighed. " There are days when I don't."

She laughed—lucky for me—and it became a cute story she'd tell family friends.

The Good Neighbor

Mr. Fleming lived two doors over in the row house on 1220 Lillian Street in Windsor. I was six when we moved in there. By the time I was eight, it was clear that I had no one to talk to, no one safe, especially in my family. I began to hang out with Mr. Fleming on his porch, as he brushed his dog, a pretty Spitz he called Sandy.

Sandy was easy to pet, easy to love. I made over her, even tried once to kiss her thin, black doggie lips. She wasn't keen on that. Mr. Fleming told me things about Spitz dogs as he brushed and combed Sandy. I told him Sandy was my most favorite dog, and someday I'd have a beautiful Spitz too. Sometimes Mrs. Fleming came out to tell him it was time for lunch. She didn't mind me being there. She'd ask me how I was doing this fine morning.

Saturday after Saturday, I spent an hour with Mr. Fleming like this. I liked him even though he was old, a little bit fat and his hair was grey and thin. I liked it that he talked to me about useful things, like how to brush and comb a Spitz properly, and what they liked to eat. I could ask him questions, mostly about Sandy.

Maybe it was more the way he talked to me, a quiet way, like he knew I'd want to know. Not know-it-all or bossy like my sister. He'd look me in the eye when he talked, but he never looked at me funny like old Joe or John did. And he never tried to touch me.

I never did get a Spitz though, or any other dog.

I never tell anyone

my fantasies of Mommy and Daddy
bound hand and foot,
gagged with strips of old sheets
hidden in a dark cellar somewhere--

my real Mommy and Daddy,
who never scream or slap me,
who never touch me in bad places
(don't tell, he said),
kidnapped by these imposters.

In the cemetery down the street,
on the grass among granite headstones,
bright stone angels and black squirrels,
I make up scenes under shady oaks and elms,

enact discovery and rescue
of my real Mommy and Daddy--
unbind their wrists and ankles,
joyful to see them
open their arms to me once more.

Night's Expansiveness

Eight years old, I lie awake
upstairs in our rowhouse.
Ilse, next to me makes
little rabbit snores.

A slice of light gliding
from the streetlamp through a tear
in the blind reminds me
of a shaft of afternoon sunlight .

I think about how, if I really looked,
I could see air. Can't be just nothing.
Must be something there.
Natural as rain. Tomorrow
I will *really* look.

The moment deepens,
a key turns within me, a door
opens—my thoughts jump
to our narrow staircase,

Why go down one
or two stairs at a time?
Suddenly I see
myself taking them all—

One Giant Step.

I *know* I can do this.
Why have I never tried?
Tomorrow I will.
Can't wait for morning.

But when it comes,
I look and look—
but find not a single
thing in the air.

At the top of the stairs,
I am dwarfed, cheated
of my night's expansiveness,
admit daylight limitations,

take the stairs one,
two at a time.
Even three
is a stretch.

The Poet as a Child

She ran barefoot at three, through summer wheatfields on the Bavarian farm, meeting red poppies, blue cornflowers and white daisies eye to eye. Ran barefoot too across the gravel road back and forth to see how many times she could before a lumbering truck reached her spot by the roadside niche of Mary, Mother of God.

At four she took off her shoes (hand-me-downs sent by cousins from Long Island) again to walk eyes closed around the lower rim, right next to the water, of the deserted swimming pool at the emigration camp, somewhere in Germany, aware that she might fall in, but just had to risk it.

She heard her first American song—*Goodnight, Irene*—on a sailor's radio the evening they boarded the Beaversbrae. For the first time she slept alone in a bunk, ate tart oranges (everyone tried to trade them for chocolate bars), threw up almost every day. Heard her new friend whisper rumors that the ship was going to sink, and was amazed to hear one morning in the mid-Atlantic that it was her birthday, and on that very same day she was five years old.

She slept in the overhead luggage net on the train from Quebec City to Regina, Saskatchewan. Ate canned chicken sandwiches and wore her best maroon gabardine dress, with pleats in front and a round white collar, for three days and nights. Uncle John met them at the station, said she and her sister would have to change their names or the Canadians would break their tongues trying to pronounce them.

She spent the winter on Uncle John's farm (his family lived in the city now), absorbing life in Canada from the glossy pages of Eaton's catalog, remembering ever after a pair of black ladies boots, trimmed with fur around the ankles. In her cousins' discarded readers, she marveled at Dick and Jane buying bananas at the grocery, and debating between red and green jello in the school cafeteria. She'd never seen a banana, never eaten ice cream, nor had a coin in her pocket. One day Uncle John gave her a silvery dime with a Bluenose Clipper on one side and the head of King George VI on the other.

She moved to Windsor, Ontario in April, when the grass was impossibly green, and the trees were budding. Tulips red and yellow, irises brilliant blue and purple. Her sister dragged her to school for the first time—kindergarten and not a word of English. She watched everyone. She watched everything. One girl wanted to trade sandwiches at lunch.

At six she played tag and hyngoseek and doctor with the kids on the street. Her best friend was Sherry, a pretty brown girl across the street. Her first kiss came from behind on her way to school when Gerry, a brown boy in her class, kissed her cheek and yelled as he ran away, "You better not tell!" Sometimes on the way to school she had a bad stomach egg.

At seven, she and her sister took a train to Grand Central Station. Aunt Pauline picked them up, took them to Long Island. (Their mother had TB , was in the San for a year). She picked up the accent easily, had to decide if she wanted it or not. Said dungarees for jeans, learned jumprope songs about the American

Beauty. Watched *Howdy Doody, Will E. Doit, The Lone Ranger* like she was born to it.

Found herself (not her blonde sister) the lady principal's pet at P.S. 37 Queens. This meant being invited to her office when there was a visitor, being introduced as "our neighbor from the north," and offered cookies. On Saturdays she gloried in roasting potatoes, telling stories in the neighborhood field with the other kids.

They returned to Windsor in June for a summer of riding in the backof their father's truck to the beach every Sunday. Their mother fixed pots of fried chicken and potato salad. They stopped at roadside stands for baskets of cherries, peaches and plums. They sang *Billy Boy* and *Der Treuer Hussar*, English and German all mixed together. The instant her father parked and cut the ignition, she jumped off, headed for the water with her inner tube. Hours later, sunburned and famished, she'd search under the trees for the family camp. Belly full, she collected bottles for two-cent deposits, for an ice-cream cone at the pavilion, where she watched the big kids slowdance to Teresa Brewer.

Holiday Scents

Cold has a white, lip-pinching smell. Boot-kicking, finger-snapping, nose dripping cold. Crystalline or powdery. Two days before Christmas, Dad and I prowl the corner Christmas tree lot. Dad hands the man a dollar for a scrappy-looking pine. At home he bores holes in the empty spots of the trunk, fits branches from the bottom into them. Smell of fresh wood, of piney sap springs into the living room, tickles my nose with anticipation. Evergreen song of joyous expectation. Mom in the kitchen mixes flour, eggs, sour cream and a splash of water for one of the two doughs to make *Hühnerkamme*-- coxcomb cookies. She makes the second dough of flour and butter, rolls them both out to the same size. Puts one on top of the other, folds them like a towel, keeps them on a plate in the fridge for an hour. While they cool, she prepares the vanilla sugar. A teaspoon of vanilla to a cup of sugar. Mixes them up, lets them dry. The subtle and sublime vanilla scent pervades the kitchen, slips into the hallway. Mom rolls the folded dough out, refolds and chills it. Three times. Her flakey pastries, filled with ground walnuts, beaten egg whites and jam promise and deliver a symphony of ecstasy. Hidden in bedroom closets, lavender soaps sneak soul-soaking vapors through cracks into our nighttime dreams. Haunting sweetness seeps and lingers. Outside frost-fingered windows, the Canadian winter sprawls in lazy wait for our snow play. Smells of ice, of snow staved off by scents of delight.

Trying Too Hard

In sixth grade someone had the bright idea of putting on a Box Lunch Auction to raise money for a school project. Girls in our class would make up box lunches, boys would bid on them. This brought up a number of anxieties for me.

Canadian kids brought lunches of white bread sandwiches with peanut butter and jelly, or with bologna and mayonnaise. In our house we always had mayonnaise and bologna. Mom bought lunchmeats at Sandwich Sausage, at the farmer's market--tasty bologna, with a touch of garlic. I'd taken a bologna sandwich to school once, and Darlene McNab came to see what I was eating. *Eew--stinky!* she said way loud, making the prerequisite face and shuddering away.

So I couldn't put our bologna into the box lunch. The other choices in our fridge were liverwurst, blood sausage and tongue, all decidedly within Darlene's *eew* factor. And who would pay much for peanut butter and jelly? Besides, we never had jelly because Mom made preserves from huckleberries and rhubarb in our garden. She also never bought Wonder-type bread. She'd get rye with caraway, Italian 'cigar' bread or pumpernickel from Modern Bakery, the best Jewish bakery in town.

The evening before the Box Lunch Auction, I puttered around the kitchen as Mom, Dad and Ilse played cards. With all of my allowance money I had bought packaged bologna, sliced cheese and white bread from Loblaws. Using mayo, instead of the unsalted butter I'd have spread for myself, I made Canadian sandwiches for two, because we'd be eating it together--me and some boy!

I was terrified that no boy would want my lunch. That no boy would want to eat with me. That Darlene McNab would come around and find something to *eew* about in front of everybody.

I cut the sandwiches into triangle quarters, wrapped them in wax paper. Lined a clean shoebox with blue wrapping tissue. Packaged cookies (not Mom's, no matter how much better they tasted), two red apples and some wrapped candy. Tying a big ribbon around the box was too girly, instead I glued Bugs Bunny and Superman cutouts over the writing on the box.

The next day we set all the box lunches on a row of desks at the front of the classroom. Mine stood out with its cartoon characters--the others were all just plain boxes. I cringed thinking of all the tissue paper I'd used to pretty it up. I don't remember who bought my box lunch, just that it was awkward. Mainly I remember trying so hard to be who I wasn't.

The Wormy Parts

At the edge of the grass, next to the onion and parsley beds,
I settle into the webbed lawn chair with a Nancy Drew mystery.
How long before my legs will tan? Mom won't be calling me
to pick tomatoes, wax beans, dill, not even to wash dishes.
She drew all the drapes, told me to go out and play
when the doctor arrived. Dad had already made himself scarce.
Ilse is just out of the hospital—overdosed on aspirin
a few days after her sixteenth birthday. Not sick,
but in bed all last evening playing Monopoly with me.

I swallow the shifting scent of ripe peaches.
Dad always pushes this small, bitten-looking fruit at me,
saying how sweet it is. I believe him and decline,

knowing I don't want to eat around the wormy parts.

Nancy Drew's life has no wormy parts. Her father
keeps an easy distance from her adventures. They go
out to supper, his hand respectful at her elbow.

Between chapters I watch the clouds smother
the August sun—respite from its muzzy heat. No sign
of tan. Sips of Coke bite at my tongue and throat.
Thoughts squirming, itching in my head,
I wonder what they're all doing
in the silent house this long afternoon.
When Mom opens the back door
my legs are turning red. For a whole week
they blister like scorched paint and peel.

Scars

We still had recess in sixth grade at Victoria School in Windsor. Sometimes we played a version of musical chairs, using the five poles supporting the long overhang by the glass doors at the back of the building. When the *It* kid stopped chanting, we'd better be hanging on to a pole, or be *It*.

This game got way rambunctious one afternoon, and I got way, way more rambunctious than I ever usually did. Laughing, screaming, yelling, squealing, we raced like crazed banshees from pole to pole. So much so that all at once I slammed into the glass door and cut a long, deep gash into my right arm. Someone took me to the hospital for stitches, then home.

The next day, Mrs. Judge, the principal, gave us a tongue-lashing. She was ashamed of us. We were hooligans. Unladylike. Ungentlemanly. She would not stand for it. We were not to play that game ever again.

At home, I still had to do all my chores. Every morning and night I had to maneuver the sofa bed I slept on, which made the wound open and bleed through the stitches. My mother seemed distant and unsympathetic, as if I'd caused her another problem.

None of us knew why I, usually pretty much a good girl, had gotten so loud and out-of-control at recess.

Could it have had anything to do with the fact that my father had gotten my sixteen-year-old sister pregnant for the second time? That she'd just had a second abortion? That Mom was taking handfuls of pills, intimating her recurring threat of suicide?

I didn't know these things at eleven, but I felt the swirl of chaotic hysteria in the house, in the family. And I still have the scar.

Walking the Fence

For years on my birthday I woke up to a "surprise" package of new underwear--Mom's best effort at a gift for me. Always included was a white cotton slip with an eyelet border across the top. By the time I was twelve, someone noticed these eyelets were as tiny windows, revealing tiny bits of my nipples and budding breasts. I did my best to ignore them, but we were still wearing the see-through nylon blouses then, so Mom and Ilse, finally said, "You have to wear a bra."

Oh no!

I was still climbing trees, playing hide-and-seek in the unfinished houses on our street. I was walking the fence across the street, trying to balance my way all around our neighbor's yard without having to jump off. A goal proper for a twelve-year-old. Mom had different ideas--now that I had my monthly period, walking the fence was no longer acceptable. "Irma-a!" she called from the front door, startling me so I lost my balance and had to jump down.

"What?!"

"You're too old to walk the fence."

I scowled at the humiliation of having to wear a stiff, white cotton, cone-shaped bra, and at the deprivation of one of my favorite activities. Not to mention the monthly horrors of trying to camouflage the bulk of menstrual cloths between my legs. How did women do it?

Having my period meant I could hang out with Sandra (who claimed she'd actually "done it"), and her bunch at recess. Telling dirty jokes. I knew which ones to laugh really hard at, I just didn't know what they meant, exactly.

These body changes--breasts and periods--brought me closer to being like Mom and Ilse. I knew this instinctively, yet not precisely. I just knew it wasn't the best of worlds. Danger lurked in shapely bods and monthly flows.

Enttäuscht.

Enttäuscht. Sehr enttäuscht, Mom emphasized. That was too big a German word for me. Given her mournful look, I could only make out that she was unhappy about something in the past. There was a lot that she was unhappy about, but this *enttäuscht* was always about this particular thing, whatever it was. Mom had dramatic ways of showing she was unhappy. I was eleven, standing in the kitchen doorway, when I first saw Mom—fire shooting out of her eyes—yelling *verdammpt* at Dad, slamming plates at the floor, flinging some at him. Dad fending them off with long arms and hands big as baseball mitts, crooning her name–*Lore, Lore*— to calm her, placate her, to implicate her with his wounded tone. As if he couldn't fathom what he'd done. No place for me to go in our small house. I slept on the fold-out sofa in the living room, and they were blocking the way to the basement where I sometimes hid. Not a time to turn on radio or TV. Nowhere. Nothing. I don't know what I did with myself. *Ärger dich nicht,* Dad pleaded. Don't be mad. But she was. In bed at night she'd fling her arm out in her sleep, smack Dad full in the head. What could he say? Years later I heard from my older sister, Ilse, that it was all about how he made her pregnant for the second time, when she was sixteen. Even Mom's threats to kill herself didn't make him stop abusing Ilse. In German class at the university I finally learned what *enttäuscht* meant. Disappointed. So disappointed. She wouldn't have told anybody what Dad was doing to their beautiful daughter. Decades later, I was cutting up potatoes to boil and mash, when it came to me: our arrival in Saskatchewan. We stayed on her brother's farm the winter of '48. Mom crying and crying over a letter. She'd left a lover in Germany and he had died. Mom, Dad and me alone in the middle of nowhere, snow five feet high as far as the eye could see. (Ilse going to school in town, learning English.) Blizzards blanked out the world beyond the windows. *Enttäuscht, sehr enttäuscht.* Where was the land of milk and honey, streets of gold? A disappointment she could tell people about.

My Thirteenth Birthday

Mom invited the ex-father-in-law
of our Greek boarder for Sunday dinner.
We didn't even know him.
She handed me a wrapped box—
a blue knitted pullover with dorky
covered buttons from neck to shoulder—
perfect for a child in post-war Germany--
I'd have died wearing that to school.
Birthday photo shows me scowling
and sulky. After dinner Mom made me
wash the dishes (as usual)
while they played cards (as usual).
I hated her (as usual).

Mid-afternoon I fled.
Nowhere to go,
no one to play with.
Walked a desperate mile
to knock on Elaine Clinensmith's door.
She didn't want to go for an ice cream soda.
Didn't want to ride bikes or rollerskate.
Didn't want to call any boys to giggle over.
Didn't want to play Monopoly or charades.
Just watch TV.
I wanted to call her dumb
and boring and stupid, so I left.
Kicked stones all the way home.

The Pear Tree

Late September, a month before I turned fourteen, Dad showed up at Patterson Collegiate, where I was in ninth grade. Three-thirty-eight by the time I came out the double-doors and saw his blue '53 Ford pick-up parked at the curb. I got in, found my old jeans and running shoes on the seat. *You can put them on when we get there,* Dad said in German, as he turned on the ignition. *There's a pear tree on the farm where I'm working. The pears are ripe now. They said we could have them all. You pick them while I finish working.* He was putting imitation brick siding on the farmhouse. We had just over two hours of daylight left by the time we got there. Biggest pear tree I'd ever seen. Huge branches splayed every which way. Easy to climb. The tomboy in me gloried in clambering from limb to limb. I filled a cloth bag over and over, took it down, emptied the pears carefully into a bushel basket. Ate just one. Picked and climbed way into dusk. A meditation-- silent, fulfilling. Picked every last pear, clear to the treetop. Showed Dad. *Fein, fein,* he said. It meant he was pleased. I could be proud. We drove home quiet in the dark, too tired to talk. Hungry. Satisfied.

Counting on Forgiveness

On the verge of fifteen, after a cousin's wedding
on Long Island, I visit relatives in Hartsdale.
A dear aunt lends a book,
The Search for Bridey Murphy,
about a woman who, hypnotized,
and the moon blazing through her eyes,
remembers a life before this one.

I read and my every hair rises to attention.
Every cell and fiber acts as if fences have fallen.
Electrified, my whole being vibrates
to a ringing, an awakening to some internal bell.
This life I lead has become too small.

Silent eddies—a mad blessedness—surround me.
Stones whirl and I cannot listen to the humdrum leaves.
I *know* this to be true, this life after life. Suddenly
I have a friend, this book, to walk with.

Will I just ask for it? Risks growl at me:
my aunt may want to keep it, maybe not hers to give,
Smoldering woodchips curl red
into grey, become the ashes of a whisper.
I cannot give it up. I dare not ask, risk
losing this book. Aching for what is real, I let go
the keening of years lost to darkness, when crows
fell out of trees and my heart was shrouded in noise.
In the end, conscience curves and shunts.
I pocket the plum. I just take it.

Taking a Stand

I was fifteen the time I made a half-smart comment, a half-sharp observation and saw Mom reach into a kitchen drawer. By the thunder across her brow I knew I'd crossed a line. She pulled out a wooden spoon. It was bad enough all the times she spewed images of me tumbling backward, blood spurting on the walls. I know now her nerves were flayed—too many secrets in her belly—Dad messing with my older sister, her own string of lovers. But what had that to do with me? Repulsed at the thought of being whacked by her incontinent fury, I skipped through the hall into the living room. She booming after, *Irma! Ich warne dich!* I had never run before. Through the dining room, into the kitchen. Round and round. She, puffing, short and fat, muddling behind. *How undignified,* I thought, *for her to chase me with a spoon—undignified too, for me to run. How long? And then what?* I turned abruptly, brought her to a startled halt. Five inches taller, I faced her. "Don't you dare hit me," I said in a low, even tone. It took a fierce moment, me staring space between us before she lowered the spoon. In the dead silence I walked out of the dining room, knowing the tables had been forever turned.

Die Rothaarige

Die Rothaarige! she'd say, disdain and fear obvious in her voice and in her eyes as they flashed from ceiling to floor, bringing this unnamed woman down to her place, where she could be managed and controlled. Sarcasm blew out of Mom's mouth that easily. She was not a creative soul--she must have heard all these potent insults which she spat out with such venom, contempt and secret terror from her own mother. Of real interest to me was -- who was this red-haired woman Mom feared so much. Who was *die Rothaarige?* I never saw a red-haired woman in our home. Never heard her named, as Sophie or Lina or Erna. No. All anonymous. And what was it that was so fearful about her! The only thing I knew about her was that she had red hair -- so that must be it. Fearful red hair. Adventurous at fifteen, I put a red rinse in my hair to augment the highlights already there. Mom's phrase with full intonation echoed and reechoed in the back of my mind. Power in red hair. Not champagne blonde waves, nor shiny black tresses. No. Red. *Red* hair meant for lust and passion. Red hair defied all. For years after that rinse had faded and grown out, I still identified my hair as auburn, clinging to the remnants of red in my hair. Knowing my mother feared it. Power in knowing how it made me different from her. *Ich bin die Rothaarige.*

A Minor Fixation

I was sixteen when I met George at Ilse and Gren's wedding. He was my new brother-in-law's school friend. Out of some need for drama in my life, I determined to have not exactly a crush, but a minor fixation on him. Dark haired, George was twenty-three, moderately handsome, though a tiny bit pudgy and not particularly tall. What impressed me was that he treated me as an equal, not just the kid sister. Maybe because I was already taller than Ilse, and could easily pass for eighteen, nineteen. As the baby in the family, I'd had my fill of not counting, of being dismissed. So this was heady stuff. As we met, he and his uncle were buying a golf club somewhere out in Essex County, not far from Windsor. That touch of glamour drew me in .

"He wants to treat us all to dinner sometime," Gren said.
"All of us?" I hardly dared hope.
"Yeah. Your sister and me, and you."

I could hardly wait. I began to plot what to wear, to fantasize what might happen, to rehearse funny lines, cool lines, anything-to-get-his-attention lines.

Early in January 1959, Ilse, Gren and I drove out to George's golf club and entered the dining room as his special guests. Me in my best Black Watch pleated skirt and forest green sweater set. Low heels, but not flats. We chose roasted chicken, mashed potatoes, gravy, green beans. Passed on frog legs and shrimp.

I glowed throughout dinner, aware I was the guest of the owner of the club. Me. (Well, I was sixteen.) George came by several times, made sure we were well taken care of. He'd sit with us for two minutes, then rush off to attend to five things on his list. By nine-thirty, the dining room was emptying out.

"Stick around," George said in passing. "We'll have the place to ourselves soon." I felt a buzz start up inside me. Just the four of us. *What could happen?*

We lingered over apple pie and ice cream. George sent highballs to round things off. I was used to drinking whiskey at home when we had a company meal or a party. Before the main course, everyone, even the children, downed a shot of whiskey, then ate a helping of cold cuts, rye bread, pickles. But only when there was company. European custom. Besides, I could pass for nineteen, even twenty-one with makeup.

Around ten George locked up, showed us around the whole place, turned the lights down low and led us to the bar.
"I'll make you some drinks. I need the practice. How about a pink lady?"

Sweet, with maraschino cherries, they went down easily as we congratulated him on the elegant clubhouse and all.

"How was that?"
"Great! What else you got?" we chimed in.
He grinned. "What'll you have?"
"Surprise me." Me being flirty.
"Okay, coming up—whiskey sours for everyone."

We drank them down with chitchat that would have been boring except that the buzz inside kept me perky. *What could happen?*

"I want to try making this thing with crème de menthe." I watched adoringly, eyes a bit glazed, as he unscrewed caps, swizzled bits of this and that into another fancy glass and slid it across the bar to me. I obliged, sipped that one down as George puttered behind the bar. Ilse and Gren went off somewhere. I didn't care. It was George and me, me and George, at last.

"How about this one? It has Cointreau and....Irma? Irma?!

Feeling a little woozy, I let myself sink down to the footbar that ran the length of the counter. Frantic, George ran to the end of the bar, looking for me.

"Are you alright? Are you okay?" He helped me up. " You sure?"

"Yeah. Yeah, I'm okay." How sweet, I thought.

"Oh god, I should stop feeding you this stuff. Let's get you some coffee."

He made coffee for everyone. Put Sinatra on the intercom and we started to slow dance on the small corner dance floor. Ilse and Gren, George and me.

Would he kiss me? Make a pass at me? What could happen? What....?

It came up all of a sudden, up and out of me—the chicken, mashed potatoes, gravy, the beans, apple pie, ice cream, the highball, the whiskey sour and the crème de menthe—out of me and all over George. Yes. All over George.

Well, that stopped all the dancing. I felt awful, nauseous. Surreal to see my throw-up all over George's black suit. He 'd have to be totally disgusted.

But they were all kind to me. Gren helped George clean up. Ilse led me to the ladies powder room, which, being out in the county, unfortunately reeked of sulphur water. So I urped again and again, wondering if Ilse was embarrassed about her kid sister. They stuffed me into the front seat of Ilse's Consul and we made our way back home.

"Irma, are you alright? Oh God. Is she alright?" George worrying and worrying. I could hear every word he said, but for the life of me, I couldn't utter a sound. I knew I was alright and my inability to convey that to poor George struck me as very funny. But when I tried to laugh, it came out weird, like a moan—and that sent George into further paroxysms of agony.

The next morning I had a total, miserable hangover, but Ilse made me eat bacon and eggs to show my father that I was alright. While it was fine with my parents for me to have a drink, being drunk was another matter.

My interest in George waned. He married, bought his wife a toy poodle to keep her company while he worked and worked.

Letter Not Sent

Dear Fred, January 11, 1961

All that summer felt like a dream come true. You'd check an art book out of Willistead Library, and hang around till my shift was done. You'd show me the paintings of Matisse, van Gogh and Renoir, tell me their stories. You took photos of me, said I was beautiful. You were cute in that badboy way I was always crazy about. But you weren't a bad boy. Sure, we'd neck and make out at the drive-in or down by the Detroit River, and god, I wanted to when you asked, but I was afraid of getting pregnant. Ilse'd had so many abortions by then, I didn't want that. You didn't get mad at me, didn't tell me to get lost. You took me to meet your mother and your little sister for tea. I learned you should never wash a teapot with soap. You were all so warm, welcoming me—strange and so wonderful.

So why did I break up with you? It sounds cuckoo, but something twisted up way down inside when you showed up wearing a bowtie to the sock hop at Herman Collegiate. An arty Tech boy with black greaser hair and a quirky sense of humor. I just I knew I couldn't go on seeing you. Not with the likes of snooty Ron Duncan and company to face in college prep classes every day. I don't remember what half truth I told you after that dance. I didn't mean to hurt you. I'm sorry. I still think about how sweet you were.

Love,
Irma

Stony Stilettos

Mr. Thorpe usually picked on Joe Clark's pretty, blonde girlfriend, Linda, in eleventh grade English class. Thorpe was from England--tall, lean and mean. He'd strut, hands behind his back, interrogating her in his clipped Brit accent. She'd stumble through, never quite getting what he was after, except to humiliate her, or maybe Joe, a many-lettered athlete. I'd watch Joe, sitting behind his girl, keeping his eyes narrowed to the text in point. I felt sad for Joe and Linda, and irritated at Thorpe's compulsive needling.

He got me once. He'd had us memorize Milton's "On His Blindness," *with punctuation,* he'd emphasized. I'd already developed that habit with Shakespeare's sonnets, so I had my Milton down. Maybe he didn't feel like hearing Linda slaughter the sonnet that morning. So when his eyes bore up and down the rows of desks, they stopped at mine, by the windows.

"Recite for us Milton's "On His Blindness," will you please, Miss Witch--with punctuation!"

Mock politeness was his hallmark signature. I felt punctuated all right. I flushed. Felt everyone looking at me. Rose to my feet, staring stony stilettos at Thorpe. Recited the sonnet perfectly. An immaculate delivery.

I sat, burning to say, "If you ever make fun of my last name (Hexel) again, Mr. Fop, I will report you to Mr. Fox, the Principal." Well, he never did it again.

Trying Again

I got a learner's permit for a driver's license as soon as I turned sixteen. My sister took me to the empty Chrysler Plant parking lot at night in our little Consul, an English Ford. I learned to shift gears, signal right and left turns with my arm out the window and parallel park. I studied the rules of the road.

When my sister and parents each took their driving tests in 50's, it was a breeze. Once around a downtown block with Murphy-- you didn't hit anything or anyone, you parallel parked within two feet of the curb--he signed for your driver's license.

But Murphy had retired. Instead of a breezy Irishman, a uniformed man with a clipboard checked off squares on a sheet as I drove. *Too many small errors,* he said, and failed me. I was embarrassed, totally unaccustomed to failing. What saved my pride was that my best friend, Marti, also failed.

Weeks later I tried again. A different man sat next to me with his clipboard. I did much better until an attempt at a left turn turned into a sudden, slow do-si-do with another car. This testing officer said, *I have no idea what that was,* and failed me.

I was in shock. The fact that Marti failed her second attempt too brought my blood back into circulation. Her father enrolled her in a professional driving class. I mentioned this to my parents, to let them know I'd be at a disadvantage now.

Bravado and pure desperation took me back to the testing office. A third man sat in the passenger seat with his clipboard. I minded all my p's and q's, dotted my i's, crossed my t's, and then the Consul betrayed me: a problem with the gearshift--something slipped out from time to time. As I was parallel parking, it slipped out.

I had to explain to this testing officer, that now someone had to go under the hood and push on a little lever way down past the engine, that I had never had to deal with this by myself since I always drove with a licensed driver. He told me to point out to him the exact lever to push. As he rolled up his white shirtsleeves, I saw my driver's license flutter away on silent wings. Marti would never have to encounter this--her family car was a regular Canadian-made Ford.

He pushed the lever, made the gearshift operative once more. We climbed back into the car. I managed a decent enough parallel park despite feeling devastated with shock and shame. I drove us back to the testing office parking lot and turned off the ignition, my heart and mind as black as the oil smudges on his sleeve.

He quietly pointed out one or two very small errors, then said I had shown remarkable calm presence of mind, for a person of my young age, in dealing with this mechanical problem. He didn't mention the oil stains on his shirt. He passed me.

I thought he was an angel. Marti passed on her third try too.

Letter Not Sent

Dear Werner, February 3, 1963

God, I'm glad it was short with you. I don't care if Dad thought we looked good together because you're tall and German. To heck with that. You conceited sleazegob, you told me you were set on having me that night in your car. No way. Fine with me that you didn't call any more.

       Good riddance,
       Irma

Eighteen

Just after five a.m. Dawn. Sitting on the curb in front of our house. Legs sprawled into the street. Only the birds chirping, and Marti beside me. June 1962. Windsor. Last day of grueling finals for grade thirteen, a maniacal if inexpensive alternative to first year university. I've already taken two English exams (comp. and lit.), two French (ditto) and the same for Latin (*"arma virumque cano..."*). Also behind me are algebra with its page-long formulae, and American history. Facing zoology today. We pulled an all-nighter—first time. Last time. Groggy and nauseous, I drag on a Cameo, inhale the menthol. Blow out the smoke. What was I thinking to try this? (sicksicksick of studying) Nothing to do now but survive coffee and breakfast, and at ten a.m. write this last three-hour exam on the amoeba and paramecium (which I could not see in the microscope), the earthworm, the fifty-three ways butterflies differ from moths, frogs (which I did not dissect), the ventricular workings of the human heart, the circulatory, digestive and elimination systems. (Sure, they left out the human reproductive system.) Already muggy. Slant-eying each other. Half-wondering— should we try blaming one another for this stupidity. Not only do I have to pass, I must earn an A in all nine subjects. Nothing counts for the whole year except these finals. I need the A's to receive a scholarship to Assumption University—the deal I worked out with Mom so I can stay in Windsor. Next week they're moving to Southfield, Michigan. I need to stay in here with my best friend (only friend), Marti. I don't know anyone in Michigan except two second-cousins who dye their Big Hair black and focus more on their make-up and fake fingernails than on any exam they ever took. Bleak. Slouched on the curb. Smoking. Head too full of zoological data, I say, *One of these days I'm going to straighten up and fly right.*

The Music Room

In 1962 my parents and I emigrated from Canada to the United States, where they bought a house in Southfield, Michigan, just north of Detroit. I helped them pack up, then settle in that summer. In September I moved back to Windsor and boarded with a German family, the Frambachs, friends of my parents. They lived about a mile from Assumption University, ideal for me to bus or even walk back and forth. My room was an oversized closet, perhaps once a baby's room, but I was glad to be in Windsor, still in daily touch with my best friend, Marti. We had both received tuition scholarships for getting an A in each of nine exams in Grade Thirteen.

I hung my clothes from hooks on the back of my door. The rest of them lived in the suitcase I carried back and forth every weekend to Southfield. The Frambachs were kind to me, took me in almost as one of their own. But the shifts, both in my family and living arrangements and in my school and work arenas, profoundly shook my sense of self. I often felt lonely, depressed or anxious in the empty moments when I wasn't occupied with whatever task was most upon me.

Many young people experience shock and disorientation in the move from high school to university. So many reading assignments, research papers due, work in the library, professors to navigate. One bright classmate, a science major, deteriorated day by day, cutting classes to play cards in the student lounge. I can't do it, he admitted one day. That scared me--he at least was still living with his family.

As French majors, we read Sartre, Anouilh and Camus, took on a veneer of lofty disaffection, marbled with newly acquired philosophical concepts. But the existential themes cut too close to the bone for me. On Friday evenings, as I drove on the Detroit ditches (expressways) from one makeshift home to the other, I found myself speculating whether I could drive through the spaces between the banks and the pillars that supported the overpasses, and make it. Closest I ever came to thoughts of suicide. A startling hallucination one afternoon in the Student Centre underlined my fragile hold on normalcy.

In my second year, the university became secular, the University of Windsor, but was still run by the Basilian Fathers. With so many changes whirling both outside and within me, I was grateful for the steadying effect of my friendship with Marti. We had discovered the three Music Rooms in the Student Centre--small and narrow, each with a record player and a floor-to-ceiling window facing the broad walkway between buildings. We'd cut the odd history class, check out LP records and listen to Joan Baez, The Kingston Trio or Ravel's Bolero, relaxing, watching students hurry or saunter from one building to another.

One day I found an LP of Gregorian Chants. I remembered studying for a European history exam in twelfth grade. Bored, I sang the facts in my notebook in my version of Gregorian Chant. I don't know where I would have heard that before--I grew up Lutheran. Curious now, I checked out the album and took it into a Music Room. The monks' voices reverberated from the cathedral in which they had sung, to the solitude of the little music room, and on into the unknown depths of my own psyche.

In moments of existential despair and uprootedness, I found refuge in these prayerful chants. They quieted my mind, my heart, even as they vibrated and reawakened a sense of something greater than this, my life as a student, greater than my current awareness of self. They transported me to a place of peace in mind and heart, which I had once experienced at fifteen, when I came to know that *in reality* I was not this body, not this person going by the name of Irma.

Letter Not Sent

Dear Malcolm   September 17, 1964

You are so weird. You think you are the cat's satin smoking jacket. Why— because of your cornsilk hair? Because you're so smart? S-M-R-T. You're not that smart, even if you did beat (barely) my tenth grade final average. You really worked for it and I just did my usual. Then you bragged about it to my mother—as if she cared. So what kind of a guy takes a girl to the movies and has his best friend chauffeur? I thought it was just one of your arrogant tricks until you had him sit between us at the movie. And what kind of guy would brag to his family about doing a lot of hot stuff with me in the back seat? Ilse was there— she told me all about it. He's gay, you know, she said. He was just using you as a cover. Well damn. But then all the rest make sense. Like when you dared me to unbutton my blouse, then wouldn't touch me. I never did anything in the back seat with you, so you'd better tell them and apologize, or else I'm through with you forever.

       Your former friend,
       Irma

Never Again

Six weeks into my summer in Germany in 1964, my best friend, Marti, flew into Hamburg to join us. She couldn't work at the General Foods factory as Jane and I did, but she was welcome to stay in our airy attic room at the Schelke's thatched cottage. Their youngest son, Karl Heinz, drove Jane and me to Hamburg to pick Marti up from the airport. From there we proceeded to his older brother's apartment to visit before heading back to the village.

We chatted in mixtures of English and German. Karl Heinz's brother, being a good host, brought out cocktail glasses, vodka and maraschino cherries to make Pushkins. Two ounces of vodka and one cherry. Chomp on the cherry three times and bottoms up on the vodka--*voilà*—a Pushkin!

We'd all had wine, whiskey, beer, if we wanted it, at our families' celebrations since we were small--it was the European way--we drank shots, always at the table with food already in front of us. We were twenty now, so grownup and the Pushkins delightful. One, two, three, down the hatch.

Jane asked for the WC. I thought that was a good idea, so I followed her, swaying slightly, down the hall. In the bathroom it hit me. Hard. I threw up. Too many drinks on an empty stomach. I sat on the floor of the bathroom and watched the floor come up, and the floor go down, and the floor go around and around. The three Pushkins had really snuck up on me.

There on the floor I vowed: nothing was worth feeling like this. Never again would I drink this much at one time.

Somehow I got myself back to the living room. Our host carried me down the flight of stairs, slung over his shoulder. My shoe fell off and someone picked it up. I felt nauseous at each bump down the steps. He stuffed me into Karl Heinz's Volkswagen bug and I suffered the thirty kilometers home.

Had a hangover the next morning, couldn't go to work. Very embarrassed in front of Karl Heinz's mother, and in front of Marti--such a welcome for her!

That was the third and last time I ever was drunk. After that I stuck to one drink, two maybe if there was food. After that it was ginger ale. These days it's herbal tea or water. Maybe once a year, a sip or two of something else.

Returning

The summer of 1964 I traveled over much of Germany, with side trips to Rome, Florence and Paris. I returned to the village in Bavaria where my family had lived as refugees after the war—the place of my first memories. We had left shortly before my fifth birthday, and now I was twenty. My friend, Marti, and I were walking past a wheatfield when a woman bicycled up and spoke to me in the thick *Bayrischen* dialect I remembered from our landlady. The innkeeper must have told her about us—we'd stopped in to pick up coffee and sandwiches.

Bist du der Hexel's Töchterin? Are you Hexel's little daughter? She addressed me in the familiar *du*, not the formal *Sie* that most Germans would have used.

Ja, ich bin Irma Hexel. Kennen Sie die Frau Heilmeier? Do you know Frau Heilmeier.?

Ach, Leid. Sie ist ja schon zwo Monat weg. Pity, she died just two months ago.

But this woman looked more curious than sad, as if my presence were an event, as if seeing me was significant news in Witzelsdorf: Hexel's daughter has returned. For my part, I didn't remember her at all. I only remembered Frau Heilmeier and maybe her half-wit brother from when I was three, four years old.

Sie haben meine Eltern gekennt? You knew my parents?

Ja doch. Wir alle haben sie gut gekennt. We all knew them well.

I was about twenty months old when we'd arrived in Witzelsdorf, summer of '45, just after the war ended. Mom, Ilse and I had spent months in a nearby castle made into a refugee camp. I had no personal memories of that time—only the stories they told. How Mom and friends had taken turns warming my bottle in their armpits. How one time I grabbed my blankie and strutted off, announcing, *Hattie gehen!* Go to Daddy. But no one knew where Daddy was, or even if he was still alive. Ilse had the scarlet fever that ran through the camp, and I the dysentery so bad I could no longer walk. Decades later I heard from my stepmother that Mom had given me Ilse's share of milk, though Tante Mila told her Ilse needed it herself. Another reason for Ilse to resent me. Why would Mom do that? To get me to sleep, so she could sleep?

They told me how Dad had tears in his eyes when he finally saw us again. We lived at first on a big farm, Mom and Dad working for our keep. But that rich farmer and his wife were stingy and mean, so Dad went across the road to Frau Heilmeier., asked her if we could live there, he and Mom would work for her. She was a spinster, alone with a half-wit brother.

"Oh no," she'd said. "At my age I couldn't stand to have kids running around here, screaming."

Dad assured her we would be well-behaved. Maybe he told her about Mom's baking skills, what she could do with a few eggs, a little butter and flour. He'd always been a good talker, so we moved our sparse belongings across the gravel road. The four of us in Frau Heilmeier's parlor. In later years I heard how Frau Heilmeier had approached Dad one day, told him how much she cared for me, that I seemed attached to her, followed her around her kitchen and farmyard chores. She wanted to adopt me—would they let her have me? I would inherit her farm. They were young, they could still have more children. They said Dad shook his head (I always wondered if he paused, considered her plea), told her he would never give away his daughter. How different my life would have been if he had!

Mom and Dad worked on her farm. Mom sold her *Hazelnusstorten* for occasions and celebrations. Dad was good at so many things that he was welcome throughout the village. He made barrels for sauerkraut and pickles. He made shoebrushes, currying brushes, any kind of brushes from the hair of horses' tails. He painted, he constructed. He fixed the axles of wagons, their wheels. He fixed roofs, rebuilt outhouses, helped cut ice from the river for summer storage. *Der Hexel.* Everyone knew and respected him.

And now this woman on her bicycle wanted a good look at me. Good that I resembled my father from head to toe—she smiled, nodded vigorously and pointed the way to Frau Heilmeier's farm. The brother was long dead, she said, and the farm already occupied by new people.

We came first to the massive gate to Thiele's rich farm. Soon after we'd moved across the road, that family had all been shot dead and robbed by a roving outlaw band, one of many loose at the end of the war. The old man had boasted too much: "Let them come—I'll be ready for them!" The robbers came in the night and murdered them all. The village buzzed with shock and horror, and no small amount of righteous satisfaction.

The gravel road I remembered well—how I'd often run across it, even barefoot, back and forth, to see how many times I could before some big truck came too close.

I would have liked to go inside Frau Heilmeier's *Farmhaus,* and to see the workshop where I'd sat on Dad's workbench, playing with wood shavings while he planed a slat of oak smooth. Where he'd built a dozen hutches, anticipating that the four rabbits he brought home would multiply. Eventually, we looked forward to rabbit stew every other Sunday or so. I remembered picking mushrooms with Ilse in the back pasture, the dry, grainy smell of the attic, full of sacks of wheat, rye, oats and poppyseeds. How I chased pigeons around the farmyard, jumped around in the hayloft, found the sled Dad built for Ilse and dragged it over the summer grass—she wouldn't let me play with it in the winter. I remembered the musty odor of hens' nests as I collected eggs, feeding orphaned piglets with baby bottles, Mom baking bread in the bakehouse.

A kaleidoscope of memories came into focus and faded. From the vantage point of the road I saw a small *Farmhaus*, the outbuildings, the yard, all hunkered down from the built-up road. It belonged to another time. A place that once lit up my life, now dimmed. A bright leaf withered. Dry. Nothing here for me.

What had I wanted—a return to the idyllic, carefree existence of my childhood?

Marti and I took our coffee and sandwiches down the road past the *Farmhaus,* to a little shrine honoring Mother Mary. My head still ballooned with images of hoeing in the fields, lunches of horseradish and salt on black bread, *ersatz Kafee*. Later, we caught the bus to Vilsbiburg, and I left forever the place of my first memories.

Taking a Stand: Road Rage

I was riding with Dad in the Galaxy, north on Woodward Avenue, on the way to Pontiac to see Mom in the hospital. I was in Michigan for the weekend, as usual. Weekdays I spent in Windsor, Canada, a sophomore at the university there. Dusk. Rush hour traffic, not too bad, but Dad started swearing at a driver who'd just cut in front of him.

He began with Romanian—familiar to me since childhood—something about the man's mother. Then Ukrainian that I knew translated into a colorful version of "up yours!" I didn't know the term then, but Dad was into road rage. He had the narcissistic view that he had all rights, that he should get away with anything he could, and others were *@/#!!•§ bastards for getting even the least bit in his way. He took every move personally.

I'd been hearing his spiel since he'd bought his first truck when I was seven. Far from being used to it, it still made my stomach curl. Now his pitch and tone escalated as he shook his fist and yelled at the driver ahead, in German now: "You cut in front of me and brake?! I'll show you brake!" He lurched the car forward. "I'll hit you!" He slammed on the brake and the Galaxy jerked to a stop. "I'll show you brake!"

Stopped at a red light. I'd had enough.

"That's crazy, Dad," I said loudly so he'd be sure to hear. "You're going to *hit* him to show him—*what?*"

Still muttering, he looked over at me.

"If you keep this up, I'm going to get out and walk."

He was silent now.

"And if you do this crazy stuff again, I will never, never ride with you again!" He blinked a couple of times, didn't say anything as he slowly accelerated and drove through the intersection. We rode to the hospital in a silent truce, never mentioned the incident to anyone.

Turned out, I never did ride with him again anyway. It just worked out that way.

Taking a Stand: Naming

Ilse and I were playing with some neighborhood kids in the huge backyard of our row house in Windsor. I remember running into our kitchen two or three times and coming out each time with a slab of dark bread, with butter and jam. Maybe they had to wait for me as we played skip or hopscotch and got impatient. I was eight, growing a lot, and must have been ravenous that day. They teased me, chanting "Chichi garbage-bone picker..." adding to it--on and on, till it was a long string of fun for them.

What stuck was Ilse calling me Chichi. I hated it and wouldn't answer. Begged Mom one day in the kitchen to make her stop. But I ran into a stone wall.

What I didn't know then was the horrendous secret that was behind the highly charged goings-on in our family the previous summer: Dad had made Ilse pregnant and they'd arranged an abortion for her when she was barely thirteen. All hushhush. Now Mom let Ilse be the boss of just about anything, including me. After a while I gave up, let her call me Chichi, which she eventually shortened to Cheech.

I was fifteen when I met Marti at the new high school in our part of town. We became best friends and eventually she also came to call me Cheech. No one else was ever allowed to call me that.

I spent a summer in Europe when I was twenty, and Marti joined me for the second half of it. We were chatting with a couple of handsome guys in Rome when Marti casually referred to me as Cheech.

Nicolo and Alessandro looked at her and said, "What did you call her?"

"Cheech. It's short for Chichi."

The two looked at each other, and by the way they then looked at me, I knew I'd had enough of Chichi forever. When we were alone, I told Marti, "Never call me that again." She understood.

A few months later, when I was on the verge of twenty-one, Ilse and her children were up from Florida, on their annual visit with Mom and Dad in Michigan. I was in my senior year at the University of Windsor and came to visit too on the weekends. We were in the kitchen one afternoon, Ilse and I at the table, when she said something to me addressing me as Cheech. My hackles rose.

Looking at her very intently, I said emphatically, "My name is Irma."

Mom stood at the sink, saying nothing.

Ilse sprang up from her seat, ran down the hall to the bathroom, sobbing as if her heart were breaking.

A Hunger for What Is Real

I lived for my children,
Mom said, her tone a mix of pride
and desperation— a belief that helped
keep her alive, let us know
she had sacrificed much.

I was nineteen,
Ilse visiting with her two boys,
three generations in Mom's kitchen.
She said it and my mind whirred,
turning and turning—

if I lived for my children,
and they lived for theirs,
where would it end—
the tail of each generation
bitten by the one after.

A hunger for what was real
hammered my heart.
I had no respite—
for whom should I live?

One day the mystery broke,
suns opened in my eyes:
live for the One
within each of us.

Live for That.

MICHIGAN, USA

Escargots

Snails, to those deprived of affectations toward *cuisine française*. That was not me when I was newly wed, newly pregnant at twenty-one —after thirteen years of French in Windsor, Canada, and a summer in Europe, including Paris the previous year. In retrospect it's not difficult to the detect signs of repressed panic: I had travelled, I had a university degree — what was I doing married? And pregnant! I'd wanted an exciting job, exotic travel, exhilarating companions! *Bien sûr, d'accord.*

Prowling ethnic markets one Saturday, I came across a basket of snails among the barrels of olives and bundles of endive. *Mais oui!* I will lift myself out of this mundane suburban existence — I will make *escargots*. I will be seen as an exotic marvel by at least one neighbor and possibly my mother-in-law. I would definitely include this in my letter to my best friend, now in Ghana with her new husband, teaching in the Canadian version of the Peace Corps. *Escargots!*

They were so small in their little shells that I bought the whole basketful, and basked in premature glory as I set them on our kitchen floor, planning to prepare them the next day. It was a good thing I bought the whole basketful — the next morning, most of the little critters were oozing up the walls, up the fridge and stove and other places I discovered two years later when we moved out of that house. *Un peu* disconcerting, *non?*

I studied the recipe I'd gotten from the library. As in any French culinary undertaking, there were many intricate steps. I won't bore you with the details, but I was religious in following them all. I collected as many of the wandering gastropods as I could find, becoming aware of a rising anxiety at the thought of tossing live creatures into a pot of boiling water. I'd heard they'd scream. *Mon Dieu!*

Perhaps I was feeling a tad more delicate than usual because I was in an expectant state — my breakfasts and I were parting company fairly quickly on most mornings. When it came to the point of this other kind of tossing, I ran to my neighbor and begged her to hold my figurative hand, so if need be, we too could scream in unison, maybe hop up an down a bit, shake off that panicky, yucky feeling of cold blooded murder. She came. *Mon amie.*

I realized then that I would never do this again. I would find other ways to inflate my ego, satisfy my need for worldly affectations, impose my *je ne sais quoi* on others. No more tossing live things into boiling water. *Quelle horreur! Trop triste.*

Like so much else in *cuisine française*, the *escargots* were required to be smothered in garlic butter. I served them with French bread and haricots verts. Invited the neighbor and her husband. He and my husband drank *le vin rouge* and gingerly chewed on one or two rubbery, black morsels. My own enthusiasm withered with each rubbery, garlicky bite. Pride made me eat till they were gone. Eat what you kill. Eat what you cook. *Quel dommage. Jamais encore.*

Burns, Scrapes and Tears

Getting ready to leave for Easter Sunday dinner with my in-laws. I bathed and dressed Stephanie, four, and Alex, fifteen months. Put him in his crib upstairs while I put on my new sleeveless, herringbone dress and fixed my hair. I was standing at the top of the stairs, holding Alex when my slick leather shoe slipped on the carpet and we started to pitch down the stairs. There was no thinking. I just did it--perhaps as any mother would--leaned all the way back as my legs buckled under me and kept Alex tight to my chest as I skied down the carpeted stairs on my shins. Cliff and Stephanie watched us land on the living room floor. A safe ride for Alex—he was hardly upset. Even my nylon stockings made it through without a tear. But underneath them I had rugs burns from my ankles to my knees. In time the shock wore off, and within a few weeks, the pain from my scrapes abated and the scabs fell off. But the sight of Cliff, even as he helped me up, trying not to laugh, trying to apologize, grinning, telling me how funny my face looked as we were skidding down, tore at something that never healed.

Strange People, Strange Things

Alex, come here. I have something for you.

I look up from the sink in Mom's kitchen to where she stands by the fridge, reaching to the top for her purse. Mom takes pills for her heart, pills for her thyroid, for headaches, backpain, blood pressure, pills for side effects and more pills for more side effects. Prescription, over-the-counter, whatever. We have an agreement that her purse stays out of my children's reach, because she keeps these half dozen or more kinds of pills in it, all bright and pretty, easy for little kids to to take for candy.

From the doorway, two and a half-year-old Alex looks interested. She calls to him again in a slightly singsong tone. He starts toward her. What does she have, special for him, as she'd said in that singsong way?

In the living room, I hear Cliff and his folks informing Dad about race relations, the recent riots down in Detroit. Lots of epithets and head-shaking going on. Five-year-old Stephanie sprawled on the carpet with a new puzzle. The family all here for Sunday dinner after a very traumatic week.

Last week I'd given Alex a couple of pieces of bridge mix candy late one afternoon as I prepared dinner to keep him from whining at me. When he started having trouble breathing later that evening, I realized there were peanuts in that chocolate covered mix. I had recently read about not giving peanuts to very young children, because they could inhale them and the peanuts would lodge in their lungs, causing pneumonia.

Our first trip to the emergency room was fruitless. Alex screamed and writhed as I held him. When the doctor asked, *Is he was always like this?* I wanted to smack him, but held my temper and explained. *Well, bring him back if he has trouble breathing again.*

And so I did the next day after a harrowing night. Never mind the details. Alex was admitted, his lungs were cleaned out, and, poor tyke, he stayed overnight for observation. Me, they sent home. Guilt and remorse wrapped tight inside me, I didn't sleep much better that night—my little son alone in a strange place, strange people doing strange things to him. With huge relief and tender care I brought him home the next day. And banished peanuts from our home.

Come on Alex, come here.

He's standing expectantly at her feet. Beaming, she draws a small paper bag from her purse. What does she have for him? I go to see. She opens the bag and pours into his outstretched hands—peanuts! I scoop them out of his hands. There is no way for him to understand. I pick him up, kiss his little hands.

And look at my mother.
What are you doing!
She all blank-faced.
I look at her as if she has lost her mind.
She blinks, gives her head a shake as if to clear it.
What are you doing?

I see the horror in her eyes—seeing how I see her. Has she lost her mind? Or is she more evil than that? I turn to the table to find a cracker, some safe tidbit to placate Alex's loss. She apologizes. Profusely. She cannot imagine what she was thinking. It will never happen again. Too late.

I know I will never trust her with Alex again. One more time, one more way it comes home to me how lost my mother is and has been to me.

The Telephone Call - 1971

Six o'clock on an October Sunday morning, the phone rang. I jumped out of bed and ran barefoot down the stairs to the kitchen phone. My husband, Cliff, stayed in bed. Our children Stephanie, five, and Alex, two, stayed asleep in their rooms.

The man on the phone identified himself as a police detective, and asked if I was Irma Sheppard, daughter of Edmund and Eleanor Hexel. *Yes.*

Something has happened here at your parents' home. You need to come right away, he said.

My thoughts raced. What could have happened? That the police were calling so early in the morning? I began to suspect--Mom.

Is it my mother? Did she try to kill herself? She'd been trying for years, since I was seven, that I knew of, threatening to throw herself into the river, taking periodic handfuls of pills.

I can't tell you anything over the phone. You'd best come right away.

Okay.

Even as I pulled on some clothes, told Cliff about the call, I knew it. I knew it.

It *was* about Mom, lying in the front seat of her Galaxie, overdosed. She'd finally done it.

The Promise

When I am big, Mutti, I will do all your work for you. Proud to be helping, I was drying dishes with my mother in the front room of Frau Heilmeier's Bavarian farmhouse, the room in which our family of four cooked, ate, slept and bathed. I was four years old.

It was a moment of closeness and contentment between us. I was chattering about what a good job we were doing, how I was getting to be a big girl, helping Mutti. I knew how to dry and put away the spoons, forks and knives.

That must have touched my mother, because she never forgot what I promised. She told it to my father later that day, and the landlady the next. I must have heard her repeat it, to have it so clear in my memory.

At seven, in Windsor, Canada, I dusted endtables, the piano, ironed handkerchiefs, towels and undershirts. I ran to the store for Mom. Eleven, I scrubbed unfinished wood floors in the house Dad had built for us. I did the dishes, dusted, ironed sheets, pillowcases and tablecloths. In the garden, I picked wax beans, cucumbers and strawberries. I picked the big, green caterpillars off the tomato plants.

Twelve, I also cut the grass, front and back, fed clothes through the washing machine wringer and hung them on the line. I cleaned the basement pantry to be ready for the summer's canning. Cleaned the whole house before Christmas, helped with baking *Hühnerkämme* and *Gipferl*, our favorite holiday cookies. Sixteen, I ironed our blouses, skirts and dresses, Dad's shirts. Washed walls and our '57 red and white Ford.

Eighteen, I packed much of our household goods for the move to Southfield, Michigan. There, I swiped the cupboards clean, unpacked and settled Mom and Dad into their new home. Mom's cousin, Erna, was impressed and jealous of how hard I work, how efficient I was, compared to her daughters. Mom bragged about what I'd said when I was four.

Weekends, I took buses from the University of Windsor to Southfield. I washed Mom's kitchen floor, windows, her Ford Galaxie. Balked at altering her clothes.

Twenty-seven, I lived with my husband and two small children in a house we were remodeling in Ferndale. I declined Mom's invitation to come wash her windows.

Twenty-eight, Mom was in the hospital again, this time detoxing from excessive intake of medications. Her kidneys were floundering. I refused to bring her drugs from home. She and Erna denounced me as heartless and useless. One month later, she had once more taken a handful of pills to medicate feelings she couldn't resolve. This time she overdosed. I declined to view her body. She never had it in her to do the emotional work that would have given her peace.

A year after she died I found myself calling for a counseling appointment. Nervous and shaking inside, I was afraid they would refuse me, saying I didn't need help. No one in our family had ever talked to strangers about the sad and ugly things that had gone on in our family. I went to counseling, went through a divorce that was as unhappy and conflicted as the marriage had been. For several years I led a double life of being a working single mom, and acting out overdue rebelliousness.

Still Safe from Blight

The elm
in our back
yard was mighty
and proud, far-reaching
branches still safe from blight.
Home to legions of squirrels, hosts
of sparrows, cardinals and bluejays, even
an occasional ambitious cat found shelter there.
Its trunk was such that it took three of us with out-
stretched laughing arms to encircle its tremendous girth.

June, July, August found us picnicking on the patio under
our elm, as it shaded Stephanie and Alex splashing in
their kiddie pool. October, it showered us with
golden leaves, which we raked into piles
knee high along the curb—the whole
street lined with gold. And bare
branches all meshed above,
created lacy patterns
under a meager
winter sun.

See Me Seamy

It was 1973. My husband and I were divorcing each other. He filed, then I filed to show I was in complete agreement. There was, in fact, a flurry of divorces in our international folkdance group at that time. On New Year's Day Doug's wife told him she was leaving him. Heartbroken, he turned to me. Not bad, I thought, an engineer at Chrysler Corporation.

I enjoyed being courted again. And since the '70s came hard on the heels of the '60s, Doug and I were soon in bed. Sadly, Doug's manly stamina was short-lived—each time. I began to wonder if this was what motivated his wife to leave him. I myself was exiting a marriage in which the marital relations had been far-flung, brief and satisfying to only one of us—not me.

Why would I sign up for another version of such discontent? The best Doug could do was to ask me afterward, *you don't really mind too much, do you?* After the third time, I understood—it was not a question.

He became critical of me when I was reading a book called *No Language But a Cry*, by a psychologist about an abused child. He demanded, *why would you read such rubbish*. My defense of the book led to sharp arguments, and I puzzled over his intolerance of my interest in this subject.

To my delight I soon met Someone Else, who had my satisfaction firmly in mind, and I firmly told Doug it was over between us. Expensive dinners at The London Broil or The Fox and Hound notwithstanding. I had my priorities.

Unfortunately, my Karmann Ghia broke down. Doug had not yet given up wooing me, and while I declined to go out with him or to "sleep" with him, I did accept his generous offer of a loan of a car. For two weeks I was genuinely grateful I had reliable transportation to go to work, to get groceries and to take my children to their activities.

On one of these outings, I bumped Doug's car into a post and dented the back bumper. On another day, I scraped a wall, leaving fender paint on it. Very unlike me. I felt embarrassed and called Doug to tell him. *Don't worry about it,* he said, still hoping for me to come around. *It's an old car.*

But then there was another bump and another scrape, and I even cracked the windshield. It just felt nuts. When I told my friend, Marty, she burst out laughing and laughing--I had to laugh too. But I kept a straight face when I showed Doug the five dings and cracks. He put a good face on it and said, *never mind,* still hoping. I turned him down just the same.

Harry Said I Should Go

His friend's apartment in Detroit wasn't new
or fancy, just solid middle America.
I wasn't the only white person there,
but it was mostly Blacks—it was the '70s
when they liked to call themselves Black.

The usual loud mix of Motown and early funk.
Red wine and white. Beer. Bourbon, if you asked.
And dope, of course. Pot—as the Whiteys said.
I must have danced. Drank wine.
But where was Harry?

In a crowded bedroom, I took a hit off the joint
passed around, and something alien crept
inside my head, scatted down my spine,
slithered and flushed around—
let it come, lie down, just let it happen—

No.

Grabbed my coat, my bag.
Headed for the door.
Hey, baby, where you goin'?
Wouldn't look him in the eye. *Gotta go.*
Hey now, what's your hurry?

Out. Down stairs.
To the Gremlin.
Found the John Lodge Expressway.

Two a.m. Every nerve bent on hurtling
through this concrete ditch.

Forty-seven minutes
of tunnelled intent.
Get home to Ferndale.
Get home to bed.
Home to crash.

Didn't think
till the next day
what someone slipped into that joint—
could've been one skanky scene.
What did Harry know?

Strings

We strung along the easy way
Stringing strings from day to day,
Weaving fantasies of love and hope.
A little wine, a little dope
Fanned the passions,
Eased the pains
That fell upon us like summer rains.

Letter Not Sent

Harry, My Man,   April 28, 1975

I was hopeless and helpless the minute I heard you laughing like some crazy man out in that courtyard at the Adult Ed conference in Ypsilanti, 1973. You gave me dope to smoke and sex like I'd never had it —all night long, you said. And the next morning you told me you were married. Well, shit. But I had to have you. You, so cool, looking so good with your Boston Blackie moustache. Black, street wise, educating this white girl, you said. Twice married, four kids, five? And you moved out on them for me. For a couple of months. When you went back to your Filipino wife, I just went nuts. Lost hope of finding a man. Going with anybody. For years.
It's good you went back to your wife and kids. You still living in that big-assed place on Chicago Boulevard? Hard to imagine you really happy and satisfied, but I hope you're okay.

    Love,
        Shep

A Bench in Piraeus

"You must come to Athens, visit us," Mary and George said in the midst of our goodbyes.

"That would be wonderful," I said. "Let's keep in touch." They had been in my beginning English as a Second Language class—Mary for at least a year, until Zacharias was born. After George had worked for two years in his family's Detroit travel agency, they returned to Athens. As we exchanged addresses, I thought, fat chance—I'm a single Mom—I don't have that kind of money or time.

Not long afterward I received a substantial income tax return, and my in-laws, newly retired to Port Charlotte, Florida, asked if Stephanie and Alex could spend a month with them that summer. Then my former husband, newly remarried and moved to Pittsburgh, also asked to have the children for a month in the summer. Suddenly I had both the time and the money.

"I'm flying to Greece this summer," I told everyone, even the mailman. Between self-images, I was at loose ends and welcomed the risky venture of travelling alone abroad. What I didn't know was how this trip was going to turn my life inside out and upside down.

Perhaps it all really started in the early sixties, when I was eighteen, dancing the cha-cha, the rumba, mambo and twist to the glorious horns at the Caboto Club every Saturday night in Windsor, Canada. "Never on Sunday" was a hot number, and by the time the movie of the same name came out, I could sing bits of its lyrics in English, German and Italian. Melina Mercouri, the big-eyed, good-hearted prostitute did her magic in the Greek seaport of Piraeus. Ah, Melina. Ah, Piraeus.

I arrived in Athens early in July, 1975.

"You and Zach and Mary will fly to Samos, near the coast of Turkey, in a few days. You will stay with Mary's mother," George said. This was a surprise.

"All the wives and children go to the islands in the summer," they told me. "For the fresh air. It's too hot in the city."

"What do the men do alone all summer?"

"They work. They go home to their mothers, to eat—or to restaurants." George shrugged, but Mary rolled her eyes, so I didn't pursue the question.

When I was unexpectedly bumped off the reserved flight early Saturday morning, they were nonplussed that I had to stay in Athens, alone with George, for the weekend. I spent the morning shopping and exploring, excited to be on my own even though it was all Greek to me. Finding a women's public toilet was an adventure in itself. (There was none. A male attendant guarded the door as I squatted in the men's pissoir.)

After lunch I took the subway to fabled Piraeus. I wandered through the market lanes, past stall after stall of fly-spotted slabs of beef and pork on hooks, then past the old waterfront jammed with sailboats and yachts. I began to feel oddly self-conscious—

because, other than pursuing the luring romance of "Never on Sunday," I didn't know what I was doing there. Tired, late in the afternoon, I walked into a park looking for a bench. When I saw only clusters of men around, I stopped. I don't know what's going on here, I thought, remembering the movie, its theme of women of pleasure. This is Piraeus.

I walked around the outside of the park until I saw some women and children and sank gratefully onto an empty bench. Made my first entry into the Greek notebook I'd bought that morning. A young Greek came to sit on the bench. Absorbed in my writing, I ignored him and soon he left. I'd just pulled out a magazine when an old Greek man sat down at the other end of the bench. I ignored him too until—

"Is that the latest *Time* magazine?"

"Yes. It is."

He wasn't Greek. American. A wiry man with gray hair. Sea-tanned. Penetrating eyes. Blue. He put one foot up on the bench, leaned back in his washworn denim shirt.

"I just saw some friends off—they're sailing to Crete. I'll be meeting them there in a couple of days. Have you been to Crete yet?"

"No, I haven't." (Crete!?) "In fact I'm flying to Samos Monday morning, to stay with friends. I was bumped off the flight this morning—kind of upset them to have me here alone with the husband."

"Oh yeah, I see what you mean." I heard some kind of east coast accent.

"I'm here for the summer. Former students invited me to visit and ...." I told him how it had all been made possible.

"That's great. Really cool," he said. "I'm passing through, on my way to India. Taking my time so I don't get there till September when the monsoon is over. My wife and daughter and I started out in Amsterdam and camped our way south. By the way, I'm Donald."

"Hi, I'm Irma. Where are they now, your wife and daughter? On Crete?"

"No. No, you see, when we got to Marrakesh, Kathy—my wife—decided she had to leave me. So that's what she did. We talked it over and decided it was best for her to take Pagan with her back to the States. That was in April. Now she's trying to figure out if she wants to divorce me."

Afterward it seemed that that hour on the bench was removed from ordinary time and space. It took place in a dimension not new to me, but rare—highly charged so every cell of my being awakened, as if to a new way of living. Donald must have brought up something about saints or gurus in India, something which led me to tell him about the extraordinary altered state of bliss I'd experienced at fifteen, something I'd never before revealed. He seemed to know what I was talking about. Who was this man?!

The sun had gone down, dusk settling in when Donald asked, "Have you eaten yet? Will you have dinner with me?"

"Sure, why not. We'll go Dutch." He raised his eyebrows at that. But, divorced for two years, I was a liberated woman. I knew the score.

Over plates of kalamari and octopus, Donald told me stories. He was the black sheep, eldest son of a Boston banking family, used to play touch football with the younger Kennedy boys, led a troop of Gurkas in India at eighteen in the Second World War, married three times, a son, twenty-two and a daughter, four. He and Kathy, twenty-six years younger, were married by a lama in Nepal. He showed me pictures.

It's hard to know now though, what he told me that evening, what he told me over the summer, after Samos and Crete, as we camped all over the Peloponnissos, and what he told me as we camped, later, across the American West for five months, and what he told me before he died in Venice Beach, California.

Donald invited me to go to a beach with him the next day.

"Love to." I could wear my new bikini.

We took the subway to Athens and somehow, under a wayfarer's moon, I found my way back to George and Mary's apartment. George's sister was there, determined to chaperone us.

Sunday morning Donald and I rendezvoused downtown as agreed. I hopped into his white VW camper, and again felt alive to his every word as he threaded his way out of the dense city traffic to a lovely beach on the Aegean Sea. I anticipated a spill of languorous summer days. This Mediterranean adventure was having its way with me.

Above the windshield of his camper, between the sun visors was a small card—on it a photo of a young man in a white robe.

"Who is that?" I asked.

"An Indian holy man," he said in an offhand manner.

What Donald didn't tell me, what he never told me was that this was a picture of Meher Baba.

Changing My Mind

I was at loose ends in Athens, waiting for Donald to show up from Crete as we'd arranged, staying at a hotel near the Plaka, making out the Greek alphabet from transliterated signs, shopping, sightseeing. One day an African man spotted me, shilled me— *pour un prix special, for you only, ma'amselle*—into entering his associate's store. I found souvenirs there for my friends—a metal-sculptured Trojan horse, a Mediterranean sun in clay, a fiery bowl painted with warriors, heroes, gods.

He caught me again as I stepped into the afternoon sun, told me he was from Kenya—*je vais vous montrer, ici une photographe—mon frère*—he is aide to Kenyan ambassador to the United Nations—you can see. A manila envelope of large publicity shots, a barrage of words, peppered with *certainement, bien sûr, vous voyez*, swept me along the sidewalk. Then about me—*vous êtes francaise? Non? Americaine! C'est bon. Vous parlez allemande aussi? Ah, trop bien.* You make a very good wife for me.

I'd been humoring this man, this cocky African, and now I was amused. *Bien sûr,* in his eyes I would make a very good wife for him, as long as I wasn't his only wife. Multilingual, educated, American...hmmm. I remembered Salim, the young Chaldean from Baghdad in my beginning ESL class: *I can make you very happy,* he repeated hopefully during the coffee break. Christian, yet Arabic in culture, to him, any woman out at night without a male relative at her elbow was fair game.

We must talk, *ma'amselle*. You must come to meet my brother. Just there, that hotel across the road. Come to dinner, *ce soir, à huit heures, bien?*

What possessed me to shrug and nod? Some invincible sense I could go anywhere and emerge unscathed?

It was dark at eight when I showed up in his lobby. He arose from a chair, looking relieved, satisfied. *Venez ici, ma'amselle,* gesturing toward an unlit stairway. Something inside me shrank. I stood silent as he urged me to mount the stairs. So dark. No one else here. He touched my sleeve. I pulled back.

No. I am not coming.
Mais, ma'amselle, pourquoi pas? Je vous en prie, venez. Venez.
No. I'm sorry. *Je ne viens pas.*
Pourquoi pas? Pourquoi?
He would not give it up.
Bonsoir, monsieur. Il faut que je rentre chez moi.

His pleas followed me past the stone-tiled steps. I fled into the safety of the tourist throng. I did not want to think what was up those stairs.

Letter Not Sent

Dear Alfredo,   November 30, 1976

Romeo and Juliet, West Side Story—that's how it was in my mind—irresistible and impossible. You looked more German than I did—blond, blue-eyed, but Dad said you were a *Lump*, a no-good bum. That was just his stuff about Italians, left over from Mussolini and the war. Werner was a *Lump*. You were just a nice guy fresh from Italy, so handsome. Later I would say you looked like Robert Redford. When I first set eyes on you I was electrified. Determined to dance with no one but you at the Caboto Club that night in 1963. Totally in love with you. At the same time I knew I would never marry you. I didn't understand any of this until years later when Donald showed me a passport photo from his twenties. He looked just like you, but with dark hair. You couldn't understand this, but somehow I knew to look for Donald in this life— eventually I met him on a park bench in Piraeus—and when you looked so like him....but that's all there was. I remember seeing in the Windsor Star your wedding announcement. I hope you had many children, a happy life.

    Love,
       Irma

Saying Too Little

It's easier for me to remember times when I said too little than times when I said too much. Once Herb, my live-in, ex-biker boyfriend slammed my seven-year-old son's head against the fridge door. I still keenly imagine how sharp pains must have exploded in Alex's little nose as he walked away crying.

I followed Alex up to his room, tried to comfort him, but deep inside I knew there were no words loving enough to truly ease the pain in his heart. Even if I'd told Herb to leave, move out, it might have been too little, too late.

It was the first and only time Herb was physically violent while he stayed with us, so it caught me off guard. But he did have an aura of tension that we all felt, and about which I was ambivalent. The Mom part of me hated it, but another part of me liked it, and used it to enhance my self-image as a tough lady who could handle anything.

I went back downstairs to Herb, said something succinct, and underlined it with a look. He never did it again.

Looking back on it, I should have said: *You need to leave. Now. Pack your stuff. Get your parents to pick you up. I don't care. I'm done. You blew it. I never want to see you again.*

When I think back on it, I see this sad event as the time when Alex determined to go live with his father. The less said about that, the better.

VENICE BEACH, CALIFORNIA

City of the Angels

I used to watch Art Linkletter's "Kids Say the Darndest Things" with my mother in the fifties. He'd mention Hollywood or sunny California at least twice every half hour. I'd wish I could be on his program, be one of the kids squirming in new clothes on one of those little chairs. I'd have told him anything he asked—a real blabbermouth—I knew stuff in my family that would've made his eyes good and round, popping right at the TV camera, so everyone watching in the USA and Canada could see—all because of what I'd said. I wasn't so little anymore when I watched his show, but I wished anyway, both for the chance to tell, and for the nifty loot the kids got. Mom loved his show and she'd laugh when a kid said something revealing. Did she ever wonder what I could tell?

Los Angeles—who first cantered north to this place and named it City of the Angels—a Spanish explorer, an adventurer, a romantic—influenced perhaps by an attendant priest? What did he see? What did he know?

When I arrived a few hundred years later, at the end of October, 1977, my head still full of images of "sunny California," the winter rains had already begun. Linkletter had never mentioned these. There was no scent of orange blossoms until spring, and then the sky turned white by noon, as if there were no weather, as if there were nothing out there, no atmosphere, at night no stars (just the moon), a vast emptiness. Except for the palm trees, the ubiquitous, cloying oleander and the Pacific, mighty and graygreen, it was almost like any other American city—miles upon miles of cement streets, asphalt freeways, strip malls, cars and buses filled with the most ordinary-looking people: Anglo, Hispanic, Black. Where was the glamour of Hollywood? Where the golden brown hills? The skyshine hype of sunny California? The sound of the Beach Boys' surfing safari?

I lived in Venice Beach, half a block from the Pacific surf, which endlessly fingered the tar spotted sands. The Boardwalk was fringed with beer-bellied bikers, long-haired Rastas, beaded and beating on their skins, bare-footed women in long flashy skirts and halters, dancingdancing to the complex rhythms. Pagan, the Poet, decked out in neo-medieval purple and lime, charged five dollars to have his picture taken with or without you. And the handsome young Black man wearing the designer rollerskates—and nothing else. It was only minutes before the LAPD had him spread-eagled over the hood of their squad car. Were they thinking to search him?

I worked as a recreation director at Hirschhorn, a halfway house on Pico Boulevard in Santa Monica. It was a zoo. Patients were being released from the state mental institution at Camarillo, medicated and sent to places like this to save money. The lunch and dinner lines devolved into the thorazine shuffle. One young man couldn't manage the relative freedom at Hirschhorn. On his first day, I arranged to meet him at the pool to get to know him, tell him what kinds of activities we offered. I found him dunking his head vigorously in and out of the pool. He apologized when he saw me, told me at Camarillo he'd be doing this in the toilet. Early the next morning the LAPD had him spread-eagled against the garage doors of the OT shop. "Hands behind your head! Interlace your fingers! Interlace your fingers!" they barked at him. They'd picked him up, streaking naked west on Pico at six am—headed for the Pacific or back to Camarillo?

City of Angels. The air was brown looking down from Mulholland Drive, the cars bumper to bumper, the land paved, cemented, asphalted—crisscrossed like a cat's cradle with freeways and interchanges. The mountains north of Santa Monica and those east of Los Angeles were visible only occasionally in February, after it had rained for three days in a row. Then the sky shone blue, the breeze bit my nose and the wave tips of the Pacific sparkled like crystals. Where were the angels?

In the spring of 1980 I came to know of Meher Baba, who said that He was the Avatar of this age. I had an inner experience that convinced me He was who He said He was. I heard or read that He 'd said that somewhere in Hollywood is the second highest spot in the world. He wasn't talking about altitude, but a place where the veil of illusion is thinner than elsewhere, where there is a certain energy, a pull. What does it mean that the veil of illusion is thinner? That karmic action and reaction are sped up? That we cycle through mental impressions more rapidly? This and more. He, the Master of illusion visited Hollywood, was feted by the stars in 1932. Film, He said, had the capacity to move hearts in a widespread, far-reaching way.

Los Angeles. The angels don't bother with city limits—Santa Monica, Venice Beach, Hollywood, Culver City, Hermosa Beach, Van Nuys, West Los Angeles—it's all city. The City of the Angels.

The Telephone Call - 1978

I'd lent Donald my VW camper so he and his seven-year-old daughter, Pagan, could drive to Boston after his mother had died. That was in June, 1978. I stayed in Venice Beach, California. I expected them back by beginning September, so Pagan could go back to school. Not a word from him.

It got hard to wait as the days and weeks rolled by. Harder to stay out of trouble. Too easy to get mixed up with characters on the Boardwalk, like Adam, the Brit roller-skater, Jack, the movie extra or Tom, the new age bookstore owner. I walked on the beach, did yoga, hung out with housemates, Becky, Rose and Bunny. Cleaned the kitchen.

By late September, after the Equinox, my nerves felt saturated with Steely Dan's new album, "Aja," that every woman in the house played day and night. Smoke of Camels unfiltered and the occasional joint were keeping me company.

The phone rang. "It's for you, Irma," Becky called up to my room. I was past hoping.

Donald. He was back. His voice took me home. My life could pick up the threads now. We had a story line to play out. He apologized for not calling me sooner. He'd be over in a couple of hours. He and Pagan moved into my room with me until he found an apartment for us. I heard his story of driving across the country and back. There was mention of a woman in Santa Monica, but that was over and I didn't care. He was back.

On the Edge: Venice Beach, 1979

August is squeezing to a close the morning
I find our quart of milk slushy frozen.
Last straw. Landlord's done nothing
to fix the fridge. I grab the carton,
march under the blackness of crows
to the corner liquor store.

> Donald, twenty years older than me,
> coughing up his lungs. Emphysema.
> His son, Richard, twenty-six,
> daughter, Pagan, nine, with us
> in two small rooms on Ozone,
> the walkway half a block from the Pacific.
> As recreation director at a halfway house
> on Pico Boulevard, I take the sometimes loony
> residents on outings all over L.A. County.
> Too often it feels like double trouble
> work in a zoo and life in a fishbowl.
> I need the freedom— make my own
> schedule, drive the van anywhere
> from Hollywood for the Merv Griffin show
> to Venice Canals where we feed the ducks.

Open the refrigerated case. Set my carton on the shelf,
take a fresh one. Reach the sidewalk but
the punky clerk says, Hey—what're you doing?
Unfoxed. Can't do this, not even in Venice Beach.
Flaming jackals. Without a word I turn around,
pull out a dollar, get change, march home.

The Unthinkable

Gary claimed to have been a co-writer of "Puff, the Magic Dragon," cheated somehow out of his rights and recognition. By 1979 that was a long-ago story. More immediate was the bullet lodged at the base of his spine. Unexploded. Could go off any moment. Never know. Dare not sit too long. Or fall down. Bullet courtesy of a robbery—he an innocent bystander.

I'd met him as I usually met new residents of Hirschhorn Manor, a board and care home on Pico Boulevard—handing him a plate of lunch and introducing myself as the recreation director. He showed up that evening in the O.T. shop to see what there was to do—which was to tell me his story. It differed from that of many of the residents, who had been medicated with Thorazine and released from Camarillo Mental Insitution. It was a pleasant relief to have a coherent, intelligent, entertaining person to talk with.

He came often and signed up for excursions around Los Angeles County. Returning one night from a Mingus jazz radio show in Van Nuys, the Dodge van died on the 405 back to Santa Monica. I put him in charge and walked a ways to phone for help. With this group I had to have rules like: no opening the doors while the van is moving. Drawing on his musical talents, he had almost everyone singing folky tunes until Ron showed up at two in the morning with the other van. Gary was so helpful, keeping our spirits up that night that I began to see him as a resident "trustee," with rights to sit shotgun on outings.

After that he was often in the O.T. shop with me. He wrote limericks about life at Hirschhorn to amuse me, tried to get me to lodge complaints against the management. Told me he had epileptic seizures—*petit mal*.

"What should I do if you have one?" I asked him.

"Just watch me," he said. "Make sure I don't hurt myself."

We were alone in the O.T. shop one Saturday evening when he said, "Feels like a seizure coming on."

I led him to a pile of yoga mats and he proceeded to writhe and squirm for several minutes. I watched intently, didn't see any harm coming to him.

He stopped, looked at me and said, "That was very courageous of you."

"Really?"

Was that for real, I wondered. That was a seizure? Never saw one before.

In my last hour on duty that night he talked to me, worrying about some kind of terrifying experience he sometimes had—a dark void—afraid he couldn't come out of it by himself. Wouldn't tell the house psychiatrist, didn't want to be put on those kinds of meds. I could sympathize with that, and he had such a persuasive tone that in an altered state of mind, I did the unthinkable. I gave him my phone number. Said he could call me if he had no one else.

As I drove home to Venice after eight that night I began to worry about what I had done. I'd never even let Hirschhorn management know I had a phone. He could call me in the middle of the night. I couldn't handle that—I desperately needed my sleep. My health was precarious—I'd just been on partial disability due to adrenal exhaustion. Helping to take care of Donald and his little daughter, living with them until recently in two small rooms—a fishbowl—working full-time in what often felt like a zoo—all had taken its toll on me. Admittedly I was not helping by smoking a few daily Camels, unfiltered, and the occasional joint.

I was off work on Sunday and Monday. Worried incessantly about Gary having my phone number, about being on call to his need. It ate at me. I remembered the first time I saw him—stepping out of a doorway on the second floor balcony. Black wavy hair combed straight back, handlebar moustache, a black coat and cane. The very image of a villain in a morality play. Who knew what he might do with my number? I was angry that he'd wheedled it out of me. I couldn't help him. I just couldn't. Monday night I rehearsed my speech, telling him I couldn't have him call me—I wasn't up for it. He had to forget my number, tear it up.

The next morning, fierce in my resolve, I went in a little before eleven, my usual clock in time. Planned to buttonhole Gary, settle this, give my anxious mind a rest.

The compound around the pool was deserted. Unusual silence hung eerie in the air. Before I reached the office to check in, Leroy came hobbling toward me.

"Hey Irma, did ya hear what happened?" He spoke clearly, almost normally.

"No, what?" What now? Weird stuff was always on the loose here.

"Gary fell off the third floor balcony yesterday." He pointed up to the railing across the compound. "But somebody said he jumped."

"Jumped!?"
"Yah. They think maybe he took some PCP."
Ringing in my ears.
"He fell on the cement over there by the pool."
My eyes followed the gesture of his chin.
"Blood all over. Awful. Blood just ran and ran. I never seen so much blood."

His eyes reflected the horror of that sight.

I stared dumbstruck, weak-kneed, struggling between that horror and the godawful, overwhelming wash of relief. My phone number was safe.

A World of Wanting

I had my fifth birthday on the Beaversbrae crossing the Atlantic in October. Regina, Saskatchewan after a three-day train trip from Quebec City, with the trunk her father made, stuffed with feather pillows, quilts to keep them warm in Canadian winters. Many hours in Bavaria spent stripping feathers off their stems, so Mutti could sew them into new bedding. No room for lovely dolls, cradles, toys my parents made for their last Christmas in Germany. But relatives presented Ilse and me with new, fancier dolls for their first Christmas in Canada.

Despite the war and its aftermath, I had never lacked for anything, never gone hungry or unsheltered. Thanks to my father's relatives in New York, we'd received boxes of hand-me-down coats, sweaters and shoes, with tins of bonbons, Hershey chocolate bars and Christmas gifts tucked in between.

Life on the little Bavarian farm had been rich--running barefoot in grassy fields, picking poppies, cornflowers, buttercups. Ilse and I hunted for mushrooms in the cow pasture. The whole family rode into the woods on two bicycles my father made, to gather blueberries. I followed our landlady as she collected eggs every morning, entertained her with my acute, four-year-old observations in her kitchen, wary all the while of the testy brood hen setting under the stove. I rode atop the hay wagon as it rolled in from the fields. We jumped around the hayloft from one level to another, swam in the river, dug for potatoes alongside the villagers, watched as men cut river ice for the innkeeper's cellar. Life was good from my three- and four-year-old perspective. Life was full, lacking for nothing.

The long prairie winter of 1948-49, I spent with my parents on Uncle John's farm, while Ilse stayed in town with his family, to learn English in school. On sunny days two farm dogs helped me explore wind-swept snowdrifts around the farm buildings. Otherwise the land was flat--white as far as I could see in any direction. On blizzard or snowy days, I whiled away the hours examining whatever my Canadian cousins had left behind in closets and cupboards—broken toys, scribbled up coloring books, crayon stubs, school readers. And last year's Simpson-Sears catalog.

These old coloring books, readers and catalogs opened Pandora's Box. I awakened to a world of wanting. I wanted my own coloring book, new, so I could color Tinker Bell and Cinderella instead of Porky Pig or Goofy, who'd already been scribbled over. From the pictures in the reader I saw goblets of ice cream, sparkling red Jello, stacks of bananas and pineapples, none of which I'd ever seen in my life. Dick and Jane and Spot entered my life prematurely. I couldn't read, of course, but in later years I put names to all these images that I pored over and burned into awareness.

The Simpson-Sears catalog was a world in itself. Little girls with ponytails in frilly pink dresses. Children riding tricycles, tossing blue and white balls. Girls jumping with skip ropes. None of which I'd ever seen. I wanted a pair of snow boots with furry lining spilling over the tops. I wanted a coat with its hood trimmed in white fur. I wanted the shiny black shoes with straps below the ankles. Page after page showed me a world in full color, a life not mine The pain of not having arose and grew. In this new country, I was a little girl who did not have.

April, we moved to Windsor, Ontario, lived on Highland Avenue for several months in the home of Joe, who rode a garbage truck. He'd wave to me from the running board as I walked to school, but I pretended I didn't see him--my first awareness of feeling embarrassed. I spent a few weeks in kindergarten, a couple of months in first grade, learned just enough English to play with neighborhood kids. My comprehension and usage picked up speed as they taught me to jump rope, play hide-and-seek and Red Rover.

Bare toehold on immigrant existence that first year. My parents found jobs. We ate decently, wore passable clothes. I had my dolls from Saskatchewan, but my new friends had so many of the things I'd pored over in the Simpson-Sears catalog. Bikes and trikes, doll buggies, skip ropes, jacks. I announced to my parents that I wanted a doll buggy. But they were too busy with survival, gave no response to my desire.

My longing for toys grew--eyes lusted for what the other kids had. Sometimes they let me play with their toys, but not for long, or ever long enough. Not mine to take home, to keep. My hands itched with desire. Outside one day a playmate was called in, leaving a pail and shovel on the ground where they'd been digging. No one else around. The thought came that I could take the shovel. I had never taken anything before, never had the thought. Now it grew on me with heat like the sun—a hot flush rose from my chest, up my neck, out to arms and fingers. I inched toward the shovel and sat on it. Mine. So easy.

I thought about what to do next. It occurred to me that I had no way of explaining possession of this shovel to anyone. I couldn't take it home, nor play with it in the yard. Someone, everyone would know it didn't belong to me. All I could do was sit on it now. My ardor cooled into guilt, fear that my attempt to steal would be seen by someone. I eased off the shovel, scooched a few feet away, pondering the contradictory outcome of desire and common sense.

On Lillian Street I walked five blocks to school, found three candy stores in the neighborhood. Two had all candy behind glass cases, but in one, all the candy was at my fingertips. I brought my pennies, nickels and sometime dimes most often to this treasure house. When my pennies didn't stretch far enough, my fingers itched to grab a five-cent KitKat. I didn't dare. But I did dare to curl fingers around three-for-a-penny blackballs when blonde Mary was busy at the cash register. Blackballs weren't my favorite, but something for nothing had a certain allure.

We moved into the house my father built on Norman Road when I was ten. My new classmates often had what I still longed for-- now it was poodle skirts and pleated silk neckerchiefs, a girl's bike. My allowance increased from twenty-five cents a week to a dollar by the time I was in high school. I babysat the kids next door, worked part time at the library. Had money for hairspray, Cameo cigarettes, a few clothes and the bus. Ilse and I would shop for bargain clothes in Detroit, across the river, Canadian dollars worth more then than the American. We tucked our purchases in our waistbands, covered all with loose jackets, rode the Tunnel bus to Canadian Customs, without declaring a thing.

My best friend and I drove to Atlantic Mills, a discount warehouse in Detroit. At seventeen we were crazy for clothes. My friend could have pretty much whatever she wanted, but despite discounts and money exchange advantages, I still didn't have enough for all I wanted. So much agonizing: this blouse or that skirt? And the temptation to take. So one time I did. Slipped a sleeveless blouse into my bag.

A dozen years later, I had emigrated to the United States, married, divorced--a single mom now. Thoroughly disillusioned regarding main-stream goals, lifestyle, ethics. Derided the smarm of Disney movies. Angry, lonely, desperate. Marijuana seemed to help. Seeking--I knew not what.

Through a series of remarkable coincidences I spent a summer in Greece, camping with the man I felt I'd always been looking for. Two years later, on a finite budget, Donald, daughter, Stephanie and I camped across the western United States for five months. I began the habit of taking an item or two extra from supermarkets. Never from small stores or businesses. I began to pride myself on my expertise, getting away with it. Robin Hood sounded good.

We ended up in Los Angeles, by the Pacific. I continued my small-time thieving, a way of life for me now. I slipped coffee and a large bar of Hershey's chocolate into my bag at a supermarket late one afternoon. Walked out pleased with myself.

One year later I was the recreation director in a board and care home in Santa Monica. It didn't pay much, but I liked the freedom to schedule activities, drive residents to events all over Los Angeles County in the van. The OT shop consisted of a converted three-car garage off the alley. A couple of long tables with chairs, a beat up sofa, a sink, cupboards and a barber's chair in the middle of it all. One day on my way to work, I found a pretty velvet pillow someone had tossed out. Dark blue, too nice to go into the trash. I took it for the OT shop sofa.

The day before Easter, I carried a huge pot of boiled eggs from the kitchen down the stairs and around the corner to the OT shop. I'd put up notices that we would color Easter eggs that afternoon and every resident would get an Easter egg on Sunday morning. Out of breath, my heart pounding by the time I set the pot on the table, I sat on the sofa to rest.

Irene came in. Short, squat, gray hair sticking out every which way, blackheads all over her face. She'd heard about the eggs and wanted one. Now. Irene never participated in any activities, never went anywhere on the van. I saw her only at lunchtime when I helped serve plates to the residents. Plaintive, Irene insisted she didn't want to wait until the next morning. She wanted her egg now. I held my ground, moved over to the pot so Irene couldn't grab one. Irene pouted as she walked around the OT shop. I ignored her, began to set up the egg-coloring project. Looked up to see Irene walking out with the blue velvet pillow.

I was furious. Outraged. How dare she!!? Who did she think she was, just walking out with stuff that didn't belong to her!!? Just because she wanted it!

I stopped short.

That's what I'd been doing for some while now. Walking out with stuff that didn't belong to me. Stuff I wanted.

I looked at how enraged I'd just been at Irene. It must mean something. This must be a message for me. I didn't want to be like Irene. I sat quiet with these thoughts. I felt a shift, a clearing inside.

I began to stop stealing. No more shoplifting. When I was given too much change, I returned it. If it wasn't mine, I didn't take it.

I began to let go of wanting.
Let longing take its place.
Longing for love, beauty, Truth.

Asking for Help

May, 1979. Things had gotten too thick for me in the apartment on Ozone in Venice Beach, California. Four of us living in two rooms and a galley kitchen: Donald, his son, Richard, twenty-six, and his daughter, Pagan, nine, and myself. Donald had emphysema, and what I desperately did not want to know was that he was dying. He was short-tempered, even mean at times in his illness, sitting or lying on his bed day and night for weeks and months, consumed with his wheezy breathing. Miserable and still craving unfiltered Camels. Too many moments bitter as spit. My name no longer safe in his mouth.

I fled to the O.T. shop of the board and care home where I worked as recreation director. The O.T. shop consisted of three garages on an alley that intersected with Pico Boulevard in Santa

Monica. The solitude was paradise. For six weeks I slept on a lumpy sofa, longing for a bed in which all my shortcomings were absolved. I used the restroom at the Burger King across the alley and showered in the Hirschhorn office bathroom on Sundays when my gay pal, David, aka Dr. Sick, was on duty. Sometimes I visited Donald and Pagan on my days off, took Pagan to the Santa Monica Pier or to play badminton for the afternoon. I still had a bed and various possessions at the apartment. I was just taking a mental health break, a leave of absence.

Though I had the solitude I craved, a profound desperation still lurked within me. I made a circlet of wooden prayer beads— blue, green, purple—for myself. With Donald slipping away, I had little left to hang on to. I had left everything—home, friends, children— to be with him. Now I held on to the beads. *Something* to hold on to, like a rosary of secret dreams as I went to sleep. I sensed a void looming, looming.

One Sunday, I locked the door of the O.T. shop and spread a plastic mat on the cement floor, between shafts of morning sunlight slanting past the edges of the doors. I wanted to pray in a way I was not accustomed to, something I hadn't memorized. I remembered kneeling at my bedside when I was twelve, thirteen, trying to say the Lord's Prayer with meaning, but the words would end up tumbling out, no matter how hard I tried to slow them down, no matter how hard I tried to mean them. I sat on the mat, crosslegged and chanted: *om nam renge kyo, om nam renge kyo*, for five minutes, maybe ten. Then, aware that I wasn't very good at this either, I stopped.

Sat between the shafts of sunlight and prayed in silence: *Whoever, Whatever is out there—please hear me. Help me. Help me. Help me.* This prayer was heartfelt, and having prayed thus, I felt peaceful. I prayed like this two or three times before Frieda, the owner of Hirschhorn discovered I was living in the O.T. shop, and said I had to leave. I moved back into the apartment on Ozone.

Beginning fall, Richard returned to Boston. Two days before Thanksgiving I took Donald once more to the hospital at four in the morning—he hacking as if to die as we were stopped at a red light. They kept him in for several days, cleaned out his lungs, so when I brought him home, he was soon able to look after himself and Pagan, walk to the beach, drive my camper.

I was on partial disability, working three days a week, due to exhaustion. My nerves were shot. I couldn't bear to hear their conversations. I found a lovely studio apartment a few blocks away and moved into it before Christmas. I bathed in the balm of solitude, of silence. I left the camper parked near Ozone for Donald's use, took the bus to work, stopped in to see them from time to time. Then gradually, Donald lost ground again, despite a new breathing/oxygen machine.

Early in March he asked me to sleep over sometimes, not wanting Pagan to wake up one morning and find him dead. She was having nosebleeds. I was seeing a skeleton's face in the mirror. I didn't sleep well there, so when Donald seemed well enough, I slept at my own place. On the first day of spring, he told me he'd broken one hundred on the doctor's scale, weighed ninety-nine pounds now.

That evening I asked him, "Are you all right for the night?"

"Yeah," he said without looking up from his notebook.

I'd been home for an hour when Pagan called, frantic. "Irma, come quick! Something's happening with Donald!"

I dressed and walked over, not in a big hurry. As if I knew. She met me at the door, pointed at the bedroom.

He lay with his head fallen into the still whirring breathing machine. I turned it off, and in the grey silence lifted him to place his head on the pillow. He did not seem to be breathing. I felt for a pulse. Found none. He had run out of life.

"Oh Donald," I whispered, holding his feet. So many dreams, so many memories of when he was wild with me, now needing to be put to rest.

I called 911.

The paramedics eventually arrived. They sent us out to sit on the steps while they pounded Donald's frail chest, hooked him up with more machines—in vain—Donald had left his body. I held Pagan after they told her, and remembered how on Thanksgiving Day we'd gone to visit him in the hospital. As we approached his room, we heard coughingcoughing and gagging and I had a glimpse of him struggling for air. As a male nurse rushed in ahead of us, I wheeled Pagan around in the corridor, saying it wasn't a good time to visit.

"That wasn't Donald," she said. "I know that wasn't Donald."

I just nodded and we left to find some pumpkin pie and ice cream.

Kathy, Pagan's mother, flew tear-swollen into LAX from Norfolk the next day. Richard arrived too. We began to sort things out.

A few days later Kathy said, "If anyone wants these pictures of Meher Baba, take them. If no one wants them, I'll take them. I just don't want them to be thrown away."

I blazed into full alert hearing those words. *She* knew about Meher Baba! I knew so little. Donald had mentioned him two, three times in five years. A poster of his smiling face had hung on the kitchen wall these past few months. I took the poster, a photo I'd first seen in Donald's camper in Greece and a book, *Listen Humanity*. A week later they all flew back to the east coast.

Baskets of bones and the blackness of pitch and ravens entered my dreams. I began to break down. I was fired from the job I really couldn't do any more, but in such a way that they were in the wrong. I collected unemployment benefits for six months, took the time to grieve, to heal and to learn as much as I could about Meher Baba. I woke up at four every morning, did yoga to a tape of harp music while it was dark. One morning, in the plough position, I hurt my neck and was in great pain. For weeks I wore a collar and had chiropractic treatments. No more yoga.

Meher Baba smiled at me from the poster at the foot of my bed: *Don't Worry, Be Happy*, it said. I didn't know how to do that, so I read *Listen Humanity*. It contained answers to all the questions I'd ever had about God, about life and death. It answered questions I didn't even know I had. One day, a knowing arose within me: *Meher Baba is Who He says He is. He is God. He was Jesus, Buddha, Krishna. It is true.* After a moment I thought, Irma, you're getting weird. You've been alone too long. But the knowing was there, and undeniable.

I dreamed of a sea otter, afloat on its back, cracking clams, fully sustained by the ocean. I dreamed true. A profound joy came over me, despite my pain and grief and fear. Meher Baba, the Ocean of Love, was here on earth just a few years ago, in my lifetime, till 1969—not just 2000 years ago as Jesus. Was here now, with me. No more Sunday God.

Months later I read Baba's full quote—*Do your best, I will help you. Leave the results to Me, I have taken care of everything. Don't Worry, Be Happy in My love.* It dawned on me that my heartfelt prayers sitting on the plastic mat on the cement floor of the O.T. shop had been answered.

The Telephone Call - 1980

Donald's lifelong asthma was much worse when he arrived back in Venice Beach. Within months it turned into emphysema. Lack of oxygen was not easy to live with-- tension between us grew. We were no longer lovers. He spent his days sitting on his bed trying to breathe, coughing, reading and writing in his very private journal. He was supposed to stop smoking. I became partial caregiver for him and Pagan, who was nine now. His grown son, Richard, helped. The four of us lived in two small rooms, with a galley kitchen, a bath.

End of 1979, Donald's strength and ability to breathe rebounded after several hospitalizations. I was on partial disability from my job for adrenal fatigue. Richard returned to Boston. I needed quiet. Peace. Privacy. I found a studio apartment a few blocks away. Left my VW camper parked nearby for Donald to use.

End of February, 1980, Donald asked me to sleep over. Didn't want Pagan to find him dead one morning. I didn't sleep well there. Too many memories. On the first day of spring, he told me he now weighed less than a hundred pounds. After we ate supper I asked him if he'd be okay for the night, said I need a good night's sleep at my place. He nodded, didn't look up.

An hour later my phone rang. Pagan shrilled into my ear, *Irma come quick! Something's happening with Donald!* I grabbed my daypack and walked over to their apartment. I noticed I wasn't hurry-hurrying. As if I knew something. Pagan was in a fright when I got there, calmed a bit when she saw me. In his room, Donald lay slumped over his still whirring breathing machine. I lifted his head, laid it on the pillow. Felt for a pulse.

Oh Donald, I breathed. Called 911 and gave directions. Held Pagan as she cried.

He started coughing and coughing. It didn't stop. He made a really awful noise. Then he yelled, 'Call Irma! Call Irma!

An Emergency

911? I have a man here who is unconscious. Could you send an ambulance right away?

Unconscious? Maybe he just drank too much.

No. No. He's had emphysema for years. He has a hard time breathing. He was trying to use his breathing machine, but he passed out.

Passed out? You sure he's not just drunk?

He hasn't had a drink in years. It isn't that. This is a medical emergency.

O-kay. We'll send a unit out. What's the address?

It's 45-D Ozone Walkway. Tell them they have to come up east on Navy. Navy looks like an alley and it's one-way, so they have to come up from the Boardwalk. I'll have someone flag them down at our building. Have you got all that?

Yes, ma'am.
Thank you.

Pagan, they're sending an ambulance for Donald. Do you want to stay here with him, or do you want to stand in the alley to watch for the ambulance?

The alley—I'll watch in the alley.

She chose the less scary of the two. I know her father is dead. I already checked his pulse, his breath. But I'm not going to tell her. Just like I didn't tell the guy at 911 that Donald is already dead. How do you know? he'd ask me. What could I say? I know.

I keep the apartment door open so Pagan can come flying in. It's almost ten at night— no time for a nine-year-old girl to be out in a Venice Beach alley. I check on her every few minutes. The ambulance doesn't follow my instructions. We see them go around a couple of times before they figure out how to get here. Pagan waves them down.

They troop in—four burly guys toting boxes of life-saving equipment. They fill up our two room apartment. They lift Donald off his bed and spread him on the floor. Start pounding his chest. It's their show now. Don't they know he's already dead?

I take Pagan to sit on the steps outside. We hold hands and talk about God-knows-what. In a while, one of them comes to us, looks Pagan in the eye, tells her her father is dead. (Has she not known?) She gasps and cries sudden tears. Of course, of course.

I don't cry until I'm sitting in the courtyard of the San Juan Capistrano Mission two days later, watching an orange balloon drift far into the blue sky.

March 20, 1980

Donald bent in a forward fall,
his head in the oxygen machine,
fingers sewn together grasp
the hose still hissing. I lift his head.
Rose-petalled blood on his cheek.
Hair so white and still. Stars hum alto
across the blackened four a.m. sky.

A small knowing plumes below
my heart. The tidy night bankrupt,
the moon hollowed. I hold his feet
unshrouded in my palms. So many
dreams, with him, now expired.
The sun's first unshadowed breath
soughs across the Pacific shore.

Passage for One

Lovers who beg respite from the heat of our dreams,
we hold on, let go by the moment—
watch Bergman once more dip her hat away

from Bogart's gaze as they stand on the dusky tarmac.
Touching knees, we read rascally Love-found Hafiz,
brush lips against each other's brow.

The goldstraw sun, having passed
over the morning stars, surrenders at last
its final embers into the farthest west.

I lie now, lax and uncoupled, still
with the timbre of your last words, watch curtains
billow into the unhoused, trackless night.

The Last Word from Your Lips

I wash the salt out of my teeth,
pocket dregs of seawater for bitter remembrance.
I watch waves carry off your eyes and lips—
your words still blowing, trying to shape me.

I pocket dregs of seawater for bitter remembrance—
we never actually spoke of marriage—
your words then blowing, trying to shape me
when we first made love, high on hash.

We never actually spoke of marriage—
though visions of your very bones enthralled me
when we first made love, high on hash.
I stand on shore now and cast your pipe--

visions of your very bones enthralling me--
far into the deepest wave.
I stand on shore and cast your pipe--
all smoking now extinguished

far into the deepest wave.
I trace yellow-grey scum on scalloped surf,
all smoking now extinguished,
remembering you lied to deceive me.

I trace yellow-grey scum on scalloped surf--
the bitterest bits dissolve into my marrow--
remembering you lied to deceive me,
they bloom as blood-roses.

The bitterest bits dissolve into my marrow.
I was the first to see your body slumped lifeless--
tears bloomed as blood-roses,
my name the last word on your lips.

First to see your body slumped lifeless, I no longer
see you set beside Orion and his splendid companions.
My name the last word on your lips,
I look to the starry backbone of my own voice.

No longer set beside Orion and his splendid companions,
your eyes and lips are carried off by waves as I watch.
I look to the starry backbone of my own voice.
I wash the salt out of my teeth.

Letter Not Sent

Oh Donald, March 20, 2001

Last words I breathed in your presence. Oh Donald. You had already left your body, but I was sure you were hanging around to see what would happen with your daughter. Pagan was nine, and the L.A. police said they had to put her in a foster home for the night because I was not kin. Kathy in Norfolk convinced them to let her stay with me. What dreams did I have left after two years of your emphysema? *Oh Donald.* I was worn down to putting one foot in front of the other. Very Zen. Very now.

Kathy flew in red-eyed the next day, to collect Pagan, and to deal with your remains, the official ex-wife. Your third. I had decided I would not be anyone's fourth wife, not even yours. You, the biggest man in my life, inches shorter than me, weighing less than one hundred pounds by that last night in 1980. My eyes stayed dry until the next day in Capistrano, sitting in the mission garden, seeing an orange balloon escape into the sky. Like you.

It was when Kathy said, *Who wants these pictures of Meher Baba?* that my heart jumped. *I do.* Like a vow. You left this for me. A new life with Meher Baba. But I dreamed of you, Donald, for twentysome years. I dreamed you were still alive, with Kathy and Pagan, not telling me. Dreamed you were still sick and weak, hiding from me. Dreamed being angry at you for smoking. Running into you, but you wandering away. Dreamed you loved me and we were okay. *Oh Donald.*

    Peace,
        Irma

He Turns the Key

1948. We were refugees in a Bavarian village after the war. Complexities following the first World War, classified us under the Romanian quota—a twenty year waiting list to enter the United States. Dad's siblings in New York couldn't help. Then my mother's brother in Saskatchewan, Canada sponsored us. We spent a long winter there, snowed in on his farm. In the spring, Dad said, *I can't make a living here.* We moved to Windsor, Ontario, where I grew up and received an excellent education.

1961. Too many bad things in our family and at seventeen, wanting nothing more than to get away, be on my own, I announced a plan go to Commercial School, be a secretary like my sister. Mom approved. It meant I'd rarely see my best friend, Marti. My only friend. I never felt drawn to any of the kids in the Commercial classes. Those girls, stationed in front of the washroom mirrors, their skirts ass-tight, plastered makeup on their faces already oozing with mascara and lipstick. I panicked. It meant university and staying dependent, but I told Mom I wanted to go on to grade thirteen.

Oh no! she shrilled at me, chin stuck out, eyes flaring. *You're going to Commercial School. You're going to be a secretary.* My heart sank. Dad, standing in the doorway, quietly said, *Let her do what she wants.*

1978. At loose ends for a summer in Venice Beach, I had an room in a houseful of women on a walkway one block from the Pacific. I didn't have a job. Sometimes I didn't know what to do with myself. I awoke one day, a clear voice ringing within me: **You**

will know everything you need to know, when you need to know it. Immensely comforting to me, this carried me through years of transition, new places and faces, new thoughts, ways of being. It comforts me still. Though I didn't know yet about Meher Baba—whose voice could it have been but His?

1980. As recreation director at Hirschhorn Manor, a halfway house in Santa Monica, I conducted activities in-house and all over Los Angeles County for the residents. Donald, ill with emphysema, was slowly dying in our tiny apartment. Helping to take care of him and his young daughter, I became depleted, on partial disability for some months. When Donald died on the first day of spring, I was too exhausted to do my job, and too exhausted to look for a different one. The new owners of Hirschhorn fired me when I refused to order a resident to clean up a barber's chair in the O.T. shop. I'd asked for a volunteer to do it, and someone in fact did clean it. Now eligible for six months of unemployment, I was relieved of my desperate need.

1980. I found temporary jobs—childcare, teaching English to a gaggle of Japanese girls. I couldn't afford the new clutch my VW camper needed, so I sold it. I felt compelled to leave Venice, but had no idea where to go, what to do with myself. People at Meher Baba meetings talked about Amartithi, the anniversary of Baba dropping His body, a huge celebration in India. It came to me all at once—I would go to India, to Amartithi. I had the money and literally nothing better to do. Time and again, Meher Baba has turned the key at crucial moments—such exquisite timing—to bring me step by step to the threshhold of His tomb.

He continues to turn the key, to direct my life, to make me His.

Cocooned in Becoming

No longer this, not yet that--
no room to turn
no way back.
Encased in this shell of not-knowing,
so contained,
yet feeling helplessly lost.
Trying to not lose my mind,
while needing to lose it.
Trying to remember
I am not this body,
not this mind.
I am in suspension.
What point of reference then?
What center can hold?

She Dreams

The man died after two years
of slowly succumbing to emphysema.
Also dead now her dream of an adventurous life.
Exhausted, she loses her job.
Injures her neck early one morning doing yoga,
and wears a collar for weeks. In pain.
Alone.
Her children far away with their father.
She misses them. She can't take care of them.
Doesn't know what to do.
Depleted.
Lost.
Rudderless.
Adrift.
No interest in living.
                How to go on?

She dreams one night of an otter floating
        on ocean swells, cracking clams open, rinsing
                them in the salt water and eating.

                She awakens and sings a joyful otter song.

Spring, 1980

I live alone in Venice Beach, California--
my children halfway across the country.

After two years of emphysema, the heart
of the man of my dreams gives out. He dies.

I am worn out, on partial disability, lose my job--
I can't really do it any more.

Yoga at five in the morning.
I injure my neck. Pain. I wear a collar.

I dream:

An otter floats on its back in the ocean,
opening clams, rinsing and eating them.

Awake,

I *know* I am the otter. Sustained.
Provided for. Safe. Content.

The man in the poster at the foot of my bed
smiles at me. *Don't worry,* He says. *Be happy.*

te quiero

                sunrise spreads
          over water
        my full-throated
          wordless lament
                  come come come
                      fiesta
                          fiesta fatal
                  heel toe clap clap
                quick quick
                  strike strike
                      turn flash whirl
                             don't forget me
                                  no   no   no
                        you won't see me cry
             this way this day
        una vez mas
                  fiesta allegria
                    fiesta fatal
            click click
          snap snap
            nadie entiende
       remember me
        just this
          swirl swirl
                I will wait for you
                      wait for you
                            you won't see me cry

Awakening

One by one I've let go of jobs,
home, friends, children,
even health, to be with Donald,

who spoke to me of You.
Now he's gone, died
on the first day of spring.

Unstitched,
I pile stone upon stone,
prayer upon prayer,

lie alone near the Pacific shore,
my neck in a brace, gazing in wonder,
Meher Baba, at your face.

Don't worry, your eyes say.
Be happy, your smile says.
I don't know how, I cry.

I read your words—they answer
all my questions,
even ones I didn't know I had.

Not just words—
Your voice rises silent and sure:
It is I. It is I.

No. I must be mad,
parsed with grief and pain,
crazed from solitude.

But Your Presence surges, undeniable,
coming from the heart of me:
It is I. It is I.

A pulse of irrepressible joy
wild within me,
a moment without shadow,

I am kissed by stars,
I am gone on God—
It *is* You.

It is *You!*

she lets go

strings it out
unbound she follows
unravels into sky
barren of double-talk
a kingdom of clouds
crowds her mind
she the leading character
but no hero
dreams and dreams
of the east--
sly undertow pulls--
the sky empties itself

Death
that come-from-behind-zephyr
parts her hair
tugs at her locks
tumbles all longing--

her skirts flown high
she empties her pockets

Arriving

I step through the open doorway—later
I remember how in that single step
an aha breathed through me.
Aha—this is the place.
A portrait, lifesize, of Meher Baba on the wall.
Fred leads a game,
naming the Avatar's favorite things--
His favorite western song—'Begin the Beguine'.
I sit in an empty row toward the back.
They are laughing.
Baba has a grand sense of humor.
I get the joke and laugh too.
Aha. I have passed through the doorway
I hardly knew I was looking for.
Adele looks at me
through timeless eyes of blue,
asks something of me—as if I knew,
as if she has known me all her life.
Meher Baba—vast enough in spirit
to be Companion to the One in each.
Ahh…

Meher Baba Caught Me

When I was fourteen, the conviction grew in me that upon receiving the bread and wine, the body and blood of Christ, I would be irrevocably altered. So it was with deep, silent disappointment that on Palm Sunday, 1958, I noticed no change whatsoever after my first communion. That September I felt electrified as I read *The Search for Bridey Murphy*. I was convinced that reincarnation was a fact.

As I lay in bed ready for sleep one night, I was suddenly in another state of consciousness. I experienced an ever-widening spiral. Blissful. At one. Whole. After some moments I returned to my normal state, but with an intense longing to recapture that spiraling bliss. I knew then without doubt that my consciousness was independent in existence of my identity as "Irma." No one understood my question: "Who am I?"

At eighteen I gave up on church. I no longer believed I would find answers to questions that arose in me. Philosophy and psychology classes seemed promising, if convoluted. Eventually I rejected all religion, believing only in the existence of God, the benevolence of His Son, Jesus, and the Golden Rule. Not that I necessarily followed their precepts.

I married, had two children, divorced, taught English as a Second Language. Former students invited me to visit them in Athens. Amazingly both time and money manifested to make that possible. I was to fly with them to Samos a few days after my arrival. But I was bumped from the flight and left on my own for the weekend early in July, 1975.

I was drawn to visit Pireaeus, the seaport where "Never on Sunday" was filmed. I had a fascination with movie and song *(Ein Schiff wird kommen,/Und es bringt mir einer,/Den ich so lieb wie keiner,/Der mich glücklich macht!)*. As I read a magazine on a bench in a park, I ignored an old Greek man until he asked me in a Boston accent, "Is that the latest *Time*?" So he wasn't Greek. Our conversation turned rapidly to matters of deep interest to me. I recounted my experience of the blissful spiral when I was fifteen. Donald, to my amazement, knew what I was talking about.

The next day Donald took me to the beach in his VW camper. I noticed a picture taped above the rearview mirror. "An Indian master," Donald said. Weeks of camping around the Peloponnesus seemed like heaven. One evening with a new awareness of love, I said, "I can love you, Donald."

He asked me to go on to India with him. I said I couldn't. I had to return to the States, to my children, my home and job there. I couldn't just disappear. But a profound anxiety seized me as I boarded the plane for the States: *I must not* lose touch with this man!

In June 1977, Donald, my daughter, Stephanie, and I set out on a five month camping trip across the Western United States. My son, Alex, went to live with his father. I had sold my house and most of our belongings.

In October, 1977 we landed in Venice, California. I was terrified at not knowing what to do with my life. Things fell apart between Donald, Stephanie and myself. In June, 1978 Stephanie flew to live with her father and brother. I felt lost. Donald and I moved into a tiny apartment with his son and daughter. Relations and his health continued to deteriorate.

I had the recurring thought that "things are not what they seem," which allowed me to go on. Sometimes I envisioned flames burning something off me. I recalled a dream I had at four: that as I stood on the bank of a dark raging river, an older boy threatened to throw me in. I'm not afraid of you. You can't hurt me." I told him boldly. "This is only a dream!"

Donald brought a poster of Meher Baba for the kitchen. I liked His smiling eyes. I found comfort in his message: Don't Worry-Be Happy. Once Donald told me something that "Meher Baber" had said. My response was "Who does he think he is - God?" To which Donald replied, "He says He is." I thought: He's God, you're God, I'm God, everyone is God.

Donald's health declined. I felt increasingly desperate, overwhelmed. My health also declined. Sometimes I prayed silently. Donald died from the effects of emphysema on the first day of spring, 1980.

Kathy, his former wife, arrived the next day. She announced, "If anyone wants pictures of Meher Baba, please take them. If no one wants them, I'll take them. I just don't want them to be thrown out." Meher Baba! She knows about Meher Baba! I thought. I took the picture I had first seen in Donald's camper in Greece five years earlier, the poster and Don Stevens' *Listen Humanity*. My eyes and ears had been opened.

In the following weeks I lost my job, injured my neck and felt utterly bereft. Children, home, health, jobs--all were gone. I stared at the poster of Baba at the foot of my bed. His message was unfathomable to me. As I read *Listen Humanity,* I found answers to questions I had had for years, and I found answers to questions I didn't even know I had.

The experience of knowing that Meher Baba is Who He says He is arose in me. I accepted this. Then I wondered, doubted my experience. But the inner knowing was such that it totally dispelled doubt. I had never had such a clear, constant experience. Profound joy flowed over me. God had *just* been on earth! Not two thousand unreachable years ago. The miraculous was not only possible, but evident in His recent advent!

On Friday, June 13th, 1980 I entered the meeting room of the Avatar Meher Baba Center of Southern California in Los Angeles. Pictures of Baba shone all around the room. People laughed as they played a game based on *The Everything and the Nothing*. I entered with the sense of having found the place that I hadn't known I was searching for. I sat and laughed heartily with the others. Moments later, Adele Wolkin entered, settled into a seat in front of me, turned around and looked straight into my heart with her blue blue eyes--looked at me as if she had known me forever.

When I heard about the dhuni at the July *Sahavas*, I knew I had to go. Smoking was affecting my health. I felt hopeless, afraid of its power over me. I was sure that my only chance was to throw smoking into the dhuni. In this way Baba took the urge to smoke clean away from me.

I sat spellbound, absorbing Baba's love and compassion reflected by the *Sahavas* guest speakers: Henry Kashouty, Charles Haynes, Don Stevens and Filis Frederick. In turn I felt overwhelmed with gratitude for the grace of being present, receiving this love, and overwhelmed with remorse over what had kept me from arriving sooner. I wept and wept.

The first time saw Baba moving gracefully, smiling, eyes flashing in Pete Townsend's film *O Parvardigar*, I was enthralled. A friend said, "Irma, you really believe this Meher Baba is God!"

"Yes!"

That evening I attended my first dhuni under a starry sky and towering pines. Sparks of Baba's Love rose crackling from the fire of Baba's Being. Love crooned from every side. Again I wept. All desire for smoking now forever gone!

I attended Baba meetings faithfully until December, 1980, when I departed Los Angeles for India. A leap of divine desperation. Meher Baba caught me, held me in His arms and has never let me go.

NORFOLK, VIRGINIA

Staving Off Detroit

It wasn't about not wanting to leave India—two and a half months there was plenty for my first time. It was just—*now what?* What to do with myself? Where to go? Certainly not back to Venice Beach, California—I was all closed out there.

On my way to India I'd left all I owned, a small trunk and a duffel bag, with a friend in Detroit. Sooner or later I'd have to go back there to collect them, but like a cat being dragged into a bath, my heart and mind yowled, *No, no, not that, not Detroit.* Which left me again with: *what to do?*

A night train with Kebi from Ahmadnagar to Bombay. A leisurely bath at Nargis's apartment there. A night flight to London Heathrow. Six days at Pete Townsend's Boathouse. He had a young Australian couple manage the floor above his Eel Pie recording studio as a bed-and-get-your-own-breakfast stopover for Baba lovers on their way to and from India. I'd spent six days there end of December 1980 and beginning January 1981 on my way to Bombay.

Now in wet, windy March, Gary Kleiner was staying at the Boathouse too. At his suggestion we took a double decker bus tour of London. How did England get to be so important and powerful that it ruled an empire around the globe, he asked me. So many levels of response possible: sea faring, lust for spices, God's will.

Liam Mullen showed up, with his current script of *Sobs and Throbs*. We shared a flight from London to New York, during which I told him I had no idea where to go from there. He didn't have any advice for me, but did empathize with my reluctance to head straight back to Detroit. I'd moved away in 1977 and hoped never to set foot there again.

At John F. Kennedy Airport, desperation prompted me to call my high school and university friend, Marti, in Ottawa, Canada. Luckily she was home, and agreed to my idea of coming to visit for a while. They had a big enough house so she and Max and their two children put up with me for six weeks. Marti and I caught up on the usual: clothes (what I had in my backpack), hair (letting mine grow long), work (my lack of), children (mine with their father in Illinois), relationships (my love interest who had died one year ago), and the unusual: Meher Baba.

Meher Baba. Having just spent over two months visiting His tomb, His home, His family and close disciples, His lovers, I felt saturated and wanted to talktalktalk all about Him. Marti and Max were skeptical. Max said, How come you know about all this and we don't.

I knew what he meant. How come he and Marti, who were solid, straight-arrow, married, professional, intelligent, enquiring, good-hearted, family people, did not know about the recent incarnation of the God-man on earth? How could it be that I, who was divorced, had numerous questionable relationships, had smoked marijuana for years, had forsaken one career after another, and apparently my children too, could merit bona fide, stupendous, spiritual connection and information that they'd never heard of?

A reasonable position--for him. I knew no answer would satisfy him. The answer that came to mind was: because I wanted and needed to know with all my heart and soul. But I never said that out loud.

Still they encouraged me to reclaim my Canadian citizenship, to make a life there in Ottawa. Perhaps they thought there was hope for me yet, that their example of solid Canadian life would help me mend my ways. But I had emigrated from Canada in 1963, moved out for good in 1965, and became a U.S. citizen in 1968. So even though the snow and ice had melted by May in Ottawa, I reluctantly bought a train ticket for Windsor, across the river from Detroit.

I called my father and his wife, Luella, and they were happy to meet my train, and take me to their home in Clawson, just north of Detroit. After a couple of days, I called my photographer friend, Norm, and asked if I could stay at his house, where my trunk and duffel bag sat in an empty, upstairs bedroom. Sure, he said.

I'd been on the move for six months, living out of my small backpack, my daypack and my sleeping bag. I'd managed to stay out of Detroit for five months, and now I was back. Knew I couldn't stay long, *but where to go?*

I camped in Norm's empty upstairs bedroom through the summer and into fall. Dan lent me his bike. Norm's wife, Connie, lent me her old car in exchange for watching her sons while she and Norm went on a photo shoot in Maine. Still no clue what to do with myself. Unwilling to try to resettle there, teach ESL again. No. I did food prep at a fast food chicken place. I talked to my kids on the phone.

One day there was a knock on the door—Norm's friend, Karl. We'd heard about each other, but never met. He wanted to hear about India. I was happy to tell him. That kept us sitting on the porch for a couple of hours. In the following weeks and months, Karl would call to ask Norm out for lunch or dinner, but with Norm not there, he'd ask me instead. On our way to the Ann Arbor Art Fair one time, Karl said, you're becoming very dear to me. At the fair, Connie's comment was, I never thought of you two as an item. Except for one fleeting moment, neither had I.

It was Kathy Hill who rescued me from Detroit. She wrote to me: "Come and live with Pagan and me in Norfolk. You can home school Pagan for sixth grade." My best offer yet. Friend, Martha, offered to drive me there. We packed my trunk and duffel bag into her VW bug and off we roared through Indiana, Ohio, West Virginia and on into Norfolk.

And just in case you're wondering, it took him six months, But Karl finally called on the first day of spring, 1982, asking, can I come and visit you? *Yes!*

Snakes & Ladders

the slow slide of snake
augurs the sporadic trail
of a lizard's tail

deep in the dust path
she is so out of being
who she once became

now a kindled soul
having shed skins of loveless life
shines as never before

The Telephone Call - 1982

I met Karl through a mutual friend in Detroit, and we spent five months getting to know each other. In October I left for Norfolk, Virginia, to live with Kathy and Pagan. I home-schooled Pagan in sixth grade, then found a job in Virginia Beach, teaching English to four young Saudi women, their husbands being trained by the U.S. Navy.

Mornings, I drove Kathy's VW Bug the thirteen miles to Virginia Beach. As I drove I began to feel caresses, as if by invisible hands, on my hair, my cheeks, my neck. While I was teaching in the Saudi living rooms, all was normal. Driving back to Norfolk, I again felt caressed, caressed, caressed. For several weeks.

I had become aware a year earlier that a man was coming into my life. Occasionally I would look into a man's eyes and wonder, *Is it you?* I'd had a moment like that with Karl, sitting and chatting on our friend's porch. But *no,* I thought. His Sufi teacher told him to marry and have children. I couldn't have any more children, and he was six years younger than me.

I'd sent Karl a birthday card in November, then a solstice card, and received no response. It seemed I was mistaken in thinking we were friends. I let it go.

On the first day of spring, a Sunday in 1982, the phone rang. I picked up the receiver and said, "Hello." I don't remember his words. But I knew his voice. And suddenly I knew who had been caressing me through the ether all these weeks.

It's you! I said emphatically.
Could he come to visit, he was asking.

Yes, yes, oh yes!

Alex, How Will I Know You?

I haven't seen you in a long time.
In photos you've sent, I see the same boy
I knew at one, at three, at eight.
Five years now I haven't seen you.

I walk down the airport corridor intent
on that moment about to come—
to see your face alive before me.
I picture that flash of reunion,
that one electric moment…

A tall young man approaches, hesitates.
Mom?

I recognize you then--my son.
Was not looking for a boy as tall as me.
Not looking yet.
Not at the gate yet.
Your plane came in early.

I was picturing how it would be.
I wasn't ready.
I have missed you too much.

A Jim Robinson Story: Lightening His Load

Toward the end of July, 1982, I caught a ride to Myrtle Beach with Jim. We'd met over several months at Henry Kashouty's Monday night Baba meetings in Virginia. On the way down, Jim talked about how his mother was ill, likely dying in Seattle, and his family was gathering there. He wasn't clear about whether he should also have flown to Seattle or should allow himself time at the Meher Spiritual Center. We arrived there late in the evening, checked in and were shown to our separate quarters. It was my first time at Baba's Home in the West.

I slept well and awoke early. Sat up in bed and heard Jim say very clearly, *Irma, there's been a change in plans.* Startled, I looked around—I was alone in the room. *What!?*

When I stepped into the Original Kitchen, Jim was there talking with a young man. He saw me and said (not to my surprise), "Irma, there's been a change in plans. These people have a light plane here and they're flying to Atlanta this morning. They've invited me to go with them. I'll catch a plane to Seattle from there. Would you drive my car back to Hampstead when you've finished your stay?" Of course.

We drove to the Myrtle Beach airport. Jim could bring only one light bag with him, so he and I stood over his car trunk, tossing heavy inessentials like spray shaving cream into an extra bag there. He laughed about how I was helping him lighten his load. It turned out that Jim arrived in Seattle just in time to say goodbye to his mother, and to connect with his siblings, bringing Baba's Love fresh from Myrtle Beach.

Mistakes I Have Made: Nothing Is Ever a Mistake

It started in first grade with Jackie Penny, who loved Maureen. Cute little towhead—I wanted him to love me, hold my hand, kiss my cheek—he'd've had to reach though 'cause I was already half a head taller than him. *Bluebird, Bluebird, in and out the window.* Maureen usually got to be the first bluebird weaving in and out of the circle, ducking under our arms. Cute in her pleated plaid skirt, her blonde ringlets. Dimples.

Here's the rest of the elementary list: Barry Burnside, fifth grade, nice quiet boy, didn't know I existed. Vitalio Roshkov—Russian. Dark curly hair, cute as hell, not too bright (usually too much to ask), and bad! The stuff of my eleven and twelve-year-old dreams, even after I overheard that sordid little exchange between him and Doris, who tended toward dowdy, and was apparently even needier than me. Then Gordon Dick. Cute, but his best feature was that he was taller than me—that counted for almost everything at thirteen—the only boy in the whole school taller than me. He knew I existed. He chased Judy and me out of a little fort we found under a poplar in the fields behind our house. We'd dressed it up with bits of moss for carpeting, a few wildflowers. *Get outta here!* Gordon yelled. *I'll knock your blocks off!* Kicked at the moss like it was icky girly stuff. We beat it. Didn't know it was his fort. Dick is right. That didn't stop me fantasizing all year about how he'd chase after me when … (fill in the blank).

Ninth grade: Ken Belanger, black leather jacket, greaser ducktail, friendly, especially to Charlene Knight, the class beauty. But he was short. Bob Nichols, however, was not. So he's the one I really daydreamed about, especially after he moved kitty-corner behind our house (even closer than Gordon Dick). A year later I had a beatnik fifteenth birthday party—black leotards, cushions and pizza on the floor—Ken, Bob, Rudy, Wayne, Malcolm all came! I have pictures to prove it. Malcolm, my sister's future brother-in-law—what a dud. Cornsilk hair, but suddenly—a total pizza-face. Smart, almost tall enough, but weird. I was halfway through university when my sister told me he was gay. That explained a lot—like why he had his buddy chauffeur us to the movies, and had him sit between us.

Eighteen/nineteen was all about Alfredo. It was *something* at first sight. I thought it was love. (I thought everything was love. That's what the songs all said.) I was enthralled. Blond, blue-eyed—looked more German than I did. Spoke no English, I picked up some Italian. Lovesick, I listened to *La Traviata*, Violetta lamenting to Alfredo, and eked out more Italian. I knew I'd never marry him, but after a year of tangos, rhumbas, chachas with him at the Caboto Club, and sneaking out to meet him on schoolnights, I let him. Twice. He married a nurse soon after, and I spent the summer in Europe where I had my first marriage proposal. Said yes, then no. Beginning to understand that I couldn't settle for a life too small, too narrow—needed room to move, to grow. Next I lusted after Alex Lukie, a Redemptorist boy at the University of Windsor, swinging his rosarie—until he left the order, swigging a bottle.

Twenty-one, I married Cliff Sheppard, a Staff Sargeant in the US Air Force. I thought we'd travel. (Albert, at the university library where I worked, commented, *How romantic.* I didn't know he cared.) Two handsome, bright children. Seven years. Eight officially because the divorce dragged on. The divorce wasn't much better than the marriage. The truth? I had no idea how to pick a man, much less love one. (I will not go into my byzantine family history at this point.)

Divorced. Two men in quick succession from the folkdancing group. They had watched the dissolution of my marriage and kept their eyes on me—one unable to get it up, the other unable to keep it up. Then, Harry! A teacher like me. Tall. Fully capable. Sexy. Handsome. Black. Married. By this time I had priorities—we had a one year affair. When he complained about the table manners of my children, I suggested he go back to his wife. He did just that. Losing Harry truly shocked me. I don't want to say what I did for the next several years. Nate, Curtis, Dan, Norm, Herb and the ones whose names I don't remember. Then Donald. This was to be a change in my love life! I thought I'd struck gold. I thought he was a keeper. (I didn't know I was his fall-back position, his last choice.) Long story short: he told me about Meher Baba. Not much. Just enough. Then he died. Meher Baba was the Keeper. He the change in my love life. *I am the Ocean of Love*, He says. *Drown in Me.*

A year later I met Karl. *Let me hold your petite little hand,* he said. How could I resist that! Married twenty-five years now. He's taller than me.

TUCSON, ARIZONA

Phone Fantasy

"Hello."
"Hey Shep, izzat you! How *are* you, girl?"
"Hey *hey*. Must be Harry! Where the heck you calling from?"

"Comin through from LA— thought to stop in sunny Tuc-son. Downtown now in this raggedyass motel. Membered you was comin here to get married. Thinkin maybe you still here. Found you in this here scrappy phone book. Now, when didja get to be a psycho-therapist? Damn, Shep, kin I still talk to you?

"What can I say? How long're you here for?"
"What's going on, girl? You still got those long legs o' yours?"
"I'm still married. How about you?"
"Oh yeah. You doin' okay, Shep? Yeah, you always okay. Damn, I miss you. I was stone pissed you didn come make love wit me that lass time in De-troit. Miss High-and-Mighty, she say, 'No-o—I'm gettin married.' Shee-it. I bin married fifty year—didn' stop me from gettin it on wich you. Didn' stop you eitha, Shep."

"Yeah, I know. I changed. Even stopped smoking dope by then."
"Kin say that agin. How old're you now, girl?"
"Sixty-one. You?"
"Don' ask. Don' wanna think about it."
"Must be close to seventy. Bet you're still good-lookin. Am I gonna to see you?"
"You wanna see me in this here raggedyass motel? You wanna see my room?"
"Mm...I'll take you to lunch somewhere."
"You still not gonna let me make love wich you."

"S'right, I'm not. But I do wanna see you."
"Why izzat, Shep?"

"Never forgot about you, Harry. Grateful as hell you left me, went back to your wife. Marriage with you would've been a mess. That year was what it was ...I still care."

"You mean that, don' you. You're a good lady, Shep. Always was. See....the way it is, is my daughta—member April? she here wit me. Had some business in LA with my brutha. Promised April I take her to see Holly-wood. She cleanin her nappy ol self up juss now. She forty-three. You believe that! How your kids?"

"So...uh... April's there...s'that mean we can't have lunch or what?"

"Well, I promised we go down to Mexico, get her some real down home Mexican cookin—caint find that in De-troit or Holly-wood, you know."

"Yeah, sure. You're—uh— not mad at me anymore?"

"Naw Shep, I'm not mad atchyou. I never forget you neitha. You in your raggedyass way o' cuttin through mah bullshit. Hey, April comin outta the bathroom. I gotta go. Maybe I call you sometime, Shep. You take care now."

My Favorite Cheap Thrill

It has to be Space Mountain at Disneyland.

In the mid-eighties Karl, friend Phillip and I visit Disneyland. We wait in lines to go aboard the pirate ship, climb onto the Swiss Family Robinson tree house, take the monorail and find some lunch. Then, Space Mountain. Phil and I are eager and antsy at having to wait in one more long line. Karl keeps saying he doesn't think he'll go on it. I shrug, but Phil tells Karl he'll like it, he has to do it just once in his life.

We finally arrive in sight of the trolley cars, and I know I want to sit in the very front car. Phil agrees. We wait for the next trolley train to arrive and empty its passengers. Phil and I sit in the front car and Karl climbs into the second one. Off we go.

My heart accompanies the trolley car in its first little lurch. A smile building inside me. We rattle past the platform into the dark domain of feigned terror. Space Mountain, a twisting roller coaster in pitch blackness, darker than night. Now a sudden lurch to the right. And downdowndown. Someone in the back cars already screaming.

I'm not a screamer. But my smile escalates to a grin, all still inside--heart, lungs stomach, grinning with anticipation of surprisesurprisesurprise!

Hard left, a semicircle, a hard right, a slow little rise, and plungeplungeplunge! Lots of screaming in the back. I'm hanging tight onto the rail in front. Eyes, ears grinning. Lurch right, lurch left, up, down, and around, around and downdown again. Omigosh. I'm in a delicious fright.

My face a grinning mask. It stays put through the remaining eternal ten minutes of plunge and lurch. A mixture of relief and regret as we trundle up to the platform, into the light. Blinking. A grin still hard-plastered on my face. Karl says he dug it too.

The Dining Room Table

Spring,
1987, I scoured
furniture stores, antique
shops and want ads for an oak
table. Compared styles, sizes, prices.
No oak veneer no new junk. Two weeks
of intense pursuit culminated at a moving sale—
a handsome turn-of-the-century table from Indiana,
a solid oak table with claw feet, to seat four, five, six.
Sushi, the little black cat that owned us, began to weave
around the great claw feet—cautious, discerning a
new threat, she sniffed and batted at them, then
washed her face in their benign presence.
Karl laughed—such an intense search
for a *table*—called me silly. This
round table—the very hub
of our family and
our social
life.

Mental Illness

At eighty-one, my father's burgeoning hallucinations caused him to believe his wife was trying to poison him, and in the middle of one night, he pressed a pillow over her face and came close to smothering her. Luella got away.

The upshot was that he moved to Florida at my sister's invitation, to live with her and her teenage daughter. The craziness in this was that he had molested my sister since before she could remember, had impregnated her at least twice, and she had already caught him molesting her daughter.

The upshot of that move was that after some months they were calling the police on each other, and my sister was nailing her windows shut so he couldn't open them to Florida's heat. Finally she put him on a plane back to Detroit.

Dad moved in with his borderline cousin and her equally inflammable husband. Less than two months later she called me saying he was pacing all night--she didn't know what to do with him. I flew to Detroit to rescue each from the other. With Luella's help, I had Dad psychologically evaluated. Alzheimer's the Doc said at first, but later changed it to senile dementia paranoia, and gave him anti-psychotic medication. His cousin tried to charge him an extra five hundred dollars to take his clothes out of her home.

Luella and I placed him into a lovely assisted living facility. I bought him a box of Kleenex for his bedside because I knew his life-long habit of spitting. But with his short-term memory all gone, he simply did what he'd always done. In less than a month, Luella was told he had to leave.

As she drove him away, he asked, *How come I have to leave this place?*

'Cause you were spitting on the floor.

Ah? They should tell me. I would stop.

Oh, they told you and told you--you just didn't remember, Luella said, laughing.

She placed Dad into a nursing home near her apartment, visited him, took him out for meals and excursions. On meds he was a lamb.

In June 1987, I visited, staying with Luella as usual. My daughter, Stephanie, and son, Alex, were living in Michigan with their father then, and they came to visit us for a day. I told them, *If Opa offers you money* (another life-long habit), *don't take it. He's taking us out for pizza later, and he has only enough money for that.*

Dad hadn't seen Stephanie and Alex in a few years, and they had grown tall into young adulthood. In the restaurant as we waited for pizza, Dad said to Stephanie, indicating Alex, *He's a good man--you stay with him.* Dad had always liked Alex, and now took him to be Stephanie's boyfriend.

I remember when I was twelve, Dad was helping me make up my sofabed in the living room. A corner of the blanket he shook out snapped at a lampshade, causing the lamp to teeter unsteadily. Angry, he said, *Who put that lamp there?!* It had been there for years, but he couldn't accept that he'd done anything wrong. It had to be someone else's fault.

I understood that I would never know if he recognized that his reaction was not normal. If I had asked, either he would be in denial of what I was talking about or he would lie. I would never know which it was. His recurring spates of paranoia generally came out in diatribes against the Jews (a dirty business), against the church (they just want money) or anyone who had ever crossed him. (stupid idiot).

I remember when I was four in Bavaria one day, my sister, her girlfriends and I were playing in my father's workshop. We fussed over the rabbits we raised for food for a while. Then the girls got silly, one by one they pulled up their dresses, bent over to show their underpants. I caught my father watching with a smile on his face that even then I knew shouldn't be there. I never forgot that smile and kept an eye on him for the rest of his life.

Most of the time he was hard-working, smart, capable, kind, generous, sociable, thrifty. When, where, why did it start for part of him to be a paranoid pedophile?

The Telephone Call - 1987

Alex came to visit me in Norfolk, Virginia in the summer of 1982, when he was thirteen. When I picked him up at the Norfolk airport, I almost walked past him. His plane had come in fifteen minutes early, so I wasn't expecting him in the corridor. And he'd grown so tall I didn't recognize him until he said, *Mom?*

That I hadn't seen him in five years was an ache in my heart. My idea of trying to reconnect with him was to do lots of fun stuff with him and Pagan. The waterslide, the ocean, sailing on Chesapeake Bay, pizza, games, picking out a new kitten. But five years' gap was too much to bridge in a week. Where was the boy who cuddled with me, told me jokes? And me--I'd also changed. Not the Mom he'd known.

I watched his plane take off into an ocean of sky, trying to hang on to some ephemeral connection with him. A sharp tug of premonition spilled into hot tears.

He was on the verge of seventeen when he came to visit Karl and me in Tucson for the Christmas holidays in 1986. We hiked Pima Canyon with friends, drove up Mt. Lemmon, ate Chinese and Mexican, went to the movies.

I kept us busy and entertained for over a week, but did no better at making that inner connection I longed to reestablish. In my heart I wanted to just hold him, hold him back to when he'd come racing in the back door to tell me a funny story. We invited Alex to come live with us after he'd graduated from high school, go to the University of Arizona. He seemed pleased, said he'd think about it.

A few months later, Alex said in the phone that he'd stay in Michigan--his father told him he could get a job that paid twenty dollars an hour. Pipe dreams. I felt sad, hopes drained. I saw him and Stephanie several times in Michigan when I went to visit my father and his wife. I met his friends, took them for pizza and ice cream.

The premonitions, the hot tears didn't stop. I prayed. Meher Baba told me to turn Alex over to His care. To not worry, to be happy in His Love. It was an order.

In June, 1987 Karl and I flew to Michigan for Stephanie's Community College graduation. Our gift to her was luggage that she picked out. She took us up on an offer to move to Tucson, stay with us. She arrived in August, got a part time job, enrolled at Pima Community College. I started graduate school at the University of Arizona.

One month later, on Friday, September 18, we were putting our dinner together around six o'clock, when the phone rang. Karl picked it up, said, *It's for you, Stephanie.* She took the phone and after a bare moment her face crumpled into tears. Without a word she handed the phone to me.

I put the receiver to my ear. It was Cliff's Aunt Ruby. *Alex.* she said. *He was in a car accident. He died an hour ago.*

Fate

In the summer of 1987 Karl and I invited my twenty-one year old daughter, Stephanie, to come live with us in Tucson. We offered to pay for her one-way ticket. The departure schedule from Detroit Metro Airport listed two flights on August 16—one around 6 a.m. and one around 11 a.m. To make the 6 a.m. flight, she'd have to get up by 3 a.m. or so, and have someone willing to drive her to the airport. I didn't want to be responsible for choosing, so I called, told her the options. A couple of days later, she called, saying she'd asked her father what he thought—not surprisingly, he said the 11 a.m. one. For some reason she decided to take the 6 a.m. flight. Her boyfriend agreed to take her to Detroit Metro.

Stephanie arrived in Tucson in the early afternoon, we happily greeted each other and drove home to begin to get her settled in with us. The next day, the news splashed over the front page of the paper was of the crash of the 11 a.m. flight, just after it took off from Detroit Metro. Everyone on the plane died except for a five-year old girl. We three felt numb, as if with shock. We tried to grasp the import—luck, fate—the slender line of life.

One month later, on September 18, we received a phone call from an aunt in Michigan. My eighteen-year old son, Alex, died in a car crash. Thrown from the car. Died instantly. A young man, high on valium and alcohol had crossed the center line in his Lincoln and hit Alex head on in his VW Rabbit.

In a daze of shock and grief, we pondered again the narrow lines of life. Alex, whose favorite game as a little boy was to play "smash-em-up" with his Hot Wheel cars. Karma? Luck?

A few days later I had a non-ordinary dream—according to some, a real meeting with Alex on the astral plane. In a state of extreme anguish, I saw Alex as he may have looked when thrown from his car—scraped skin, bones sticking out. But he was smiling at me with great love, as if to say, *It's okay Mom. It had to happen. I did good.* His face was shining.

Letter Not Sent

Dear Cliff, August 13, 1997

I thought you were a nerd when you asked me to dance at that club in Detroit. 1964—if I hadn't been so desperately lonely, I would not have gone to see *Topkapi* with you the next weekend. I know now I married you for "social security." I don't know why you married me. Maybe it was fate. We worked and played hard— remodeling our house in Ferndale, Michigan, painting Easter eggs for the kids, making gingerbread houses to sell at Christmas, folkdancing. But for all that we were hurt and angry, blaming each other and not knowing how to love. We just played house. That's the nutshell synopsis. When we split up after seven years, our divorce was just as miserable as our marriage. I remember my first haircut after you moved out, how the hairdresser said my stomach was all relaxed now. *How can you tell*, I asked him.

Alex is gone, died in a car crash. Stephanie told me she stopped contact with you because you were disrespectful about me. I heard you're not in touch with your other daughter either. I think about you on the holidays, birthdays, death-days—did you know your father died? I'm sad for you. For me, I'm just relieved you're out of my life.

    Best wishes,
        Irma

Ashes, Ashes

I kept Mom's ashes in a cardboard box in my Ferndale, Michigan basement until Dad took them to Opa-Locka, Florida when he went to live with my sister, Ilse. She buried Mom's ashes in her backyard. Twenty-some years later, when Dad flew down there to try to live with her again (both times ended in disaster), they moved to Waycross, Georgia. She dug up Mom's ashes and reburied them in Waycross.

Through these years I'd moved from Ferndale to Venice Beach, to India, to Michigan, to Norfolk, Virginia to Tucson, Arizona, all of which left me with neither interest nor objection to Ilse's burials and exhumation of Mom's ashes. She seemed settled in Waycross, and that was fine with me.

On one of my visits to see Dad in Michigan, his wife, Luella, took us on a jaunt out into the countryside. We stopped by a shaded old cemetery, pored over names and dates on tilted, blackened headstones. At the edge of a nearby pond Dad and I watched ducks paddle and dive. Dad at eighty-one had lived longer than his parents and his siblings had.

Where do you want to be buried when you die? I asked.
In the ground. He smirked at his joke.
Okay. Here in Michigan or in Georgia with Mom?
Here, there--es ist mir egal, he said. All the same to him.

I remembered how he hadn't liked Georgia when he lived there with Ilse. The *grass is sour*, he said. *No good for horses*. Ilse must have been talking about getting a horse. It was the face he made--*sour*--when he said that. Like he wouldn't want even his ashes to be buried in sour soil.

Luella had been good to him for years, through all his senile dementia paranoia, and violence. When he died at eighty-six, she had him cremated, said she had a space for him next to her in Royal Oak, Michigan, her first husband on her other side.

That's fine, I said.

He'd lived in Michigan for twenty-seven years. My son was already buried there. What did Dad have in Georgia except Mom's ashes? By the time he died Ilse was already not speaking to me, so I didn't worry about what she would say. Luella didn't ask her either. It was one more reason for Ilse to be mad at me.

Come to India with Me

1975

"Come to India with me," Donald said. Camped in Olympia on the Peleponnesus, we sat smoking under the dusky olive trees.

My mind went blank, unwilling to entertain images of abandoned children, outraged relatives, bewildered friends. "I can't," I said. "I have two children, a house and a job back in Michigan. I can't just disappear." How would I have lived with myself?

1980

Donald died in Venice Beach, California on the first day of spring. Emphysema. I had sold my house and left my job in Michigan in 1977. Alex, and a year later, Stephanie had gone to live with their father in Illinois. In helping to care for Donald and his young daughter, working full-time—and still smoking—I'd lost my health. After he died I lost my job and injured my neck. Broke, alone, in pain, I read *Listen Humanity* and came to know from a deep solitude that Meher Baba is the Avatar of the Age, the One I had always longed for. Months later, I sold my camper, used the money to fly to His tomb in India. By myself.

1991

Stephanie and I visited Fort Daulatabad, near Aurangabad on the Deccan Plateau in India, with a few other pilgrims. Line after line of fortifications made it impregnable except by means of internal betrayal. I had lagged and found myself separated from the others, alone with an Indian guide in a tunnel. We stood directly under a rectangular opening through which defenders had poured boiling oil on the heads of their invaders.

"Come," said the guide, and walked me away from the sunlit opening. The tunnel darkened gradually, then dramatically. Ahead it was dark—and only that. Neither he nor I had a torch.

"Wait," I said.
"Come." He held his hand out to me.
"No!" I shrank back toward the last bit of light.
"Don't worry," he said, looking at me intently. "*Don't worry.*"

Meher Baba's own words. They resonated within me and reassured me. I took his hand and turned with him into the pitch dark air with small stuttering steps. Black into black into black until at last, *at last* it lightened just enough to allow the breath to leave my throat more freely, and turning, we stood again—in his triumphant gaze—under the very opening where Marathi defenders of the thirteenth century had desperately poured scalding oil on Moghul attackers.

"See!" he said. "They go this way—same. They go that way—same. They always come to this spot—where is sunlight. Then—boiling oil.

What if I had gone directly to India with Donald? The longer road I ended up taking was dotted with adventure, exhilaration, new freedoms and self-discovery, as well as mishaps, losses, pain and sorrow. I go this way—same. I go that way—same. Boiling oil. Meher Baba's love.

Running Late

My husband, Karl, and I had agreed to meet at the tax accountant's office for our appointment with her to begin our annual tax process. In plenty of time I drove to her office only to find it shut and empty. Oh! That's right--they moved their office. I racked my brain to remember their new location. Yes, I got it. Started the car and pulled back into heavy mid-afternoon traffic.

Hit red lights one after another. Pokey drivers not getting a move-on. Was I going to be late? I didn't like to be late. Probably part of my good girl self-image dating back to early childhood. Small waves of tension crept across my shoulders, up into my neck. Dull ache in my head. Small knots connecting in my stomach. Stuck with cars all around me.

Karl should have reminded me. He's the one who told me they moved to a new location. If I was late, it would be because of him. He should have reminded me. It was his fault. And I had all the tax papers with me. These ruminations circled in my head for a block and a half. At the next red light, it hit me.

How hard I was working to pin it on him! My old habit. Learned all the years in my family--*it's not my fault!* But this was. I was responsible. Now watching how my mind twisted to turn myself innocent. A victim, even. Oh dear. *No.*

A turning point here in my relationship with myself. Alive with a new sense of self, I was ten minutes late. I apologized and owned up to driving to the old office site. No big deal.

The Telephone Call -- 1988

About a year after Alex died, I was home alone when the phone rang. It was a lawyer in Michigan. Cliff had engaged him for a wrongful death suit against the man who crashed his Lincoln head on into Alex's Rabbit. The lawyer explained the legal suit to me. He stated that, as I was Alex's mother, I was entitled to participate in this legal action, and receive some of the money that would be awarded. He said they were going after the young man's insurance and also that of the tavern where he had mixed alcohol with Valium.

I listened, a horror welling up within me.
"Do you want to participate in this suit?" he finally asked.
I bent over, doubled up, sank to the kitchen floor.
"No! No, no, no!! I screamed, as if all the way up to Michigan.

As if he would understand that I would not accept blood money for the loss of my son. It was Cliff's way to deal with his hurt, his anger like this, not mine.

"Well, you can think about it. We'll send you the forms to fill out," he concluded.

I hung up, bereft anew.

When I next saw my therapist, she took me through to see the situation rationally. It was money. I was entitled. I filled out the forms and signed them.

I used the money I received toward my graduate degree. After I graduated, I spent two months at Meher Baba's Pilgrim Center in India with Stephanie. I used part of this money to set myself up as a therapist in private practice. I bought some handsome living room furniture, refurbished an antique oak dining table. The last thousand I spent on Stephanie's move to Champaign, Illinois, where she had a scholarship for a graduate fine arts program.

I was grateful to be able to do all this.

A Sign from Baba

October 22 is my birth date. In 1981 I read in India that 22 is a master number. I don't know exactly what that means, just that it and 222 have great significance for me. Sighting them, I sometimes take them as a sign, and always take them as a moment in which to say, *Yes, Baba*.

I remember the time in August 1991, when my daughter, Stephanie, 25, and I were leaving the Pilgrim Center at Meherabad, India. Gayle— new to Baba, and not yet convinced of His claim to divinity, but totally convinced she'd be terrified traveling alone in India—was riding with us to the Bombay airport.

I had my own travails, doubts and worries. Traveling in India is never a sure thing. On our taxi ride from Bombay to Ahmednagar two months earlier, Stephanie and I had had the opportunity to summon and exercise newfound depths of faith and surrender. By the time we'd reached the open road of the countryside, we'd narrowly missed dozens of Tata trucks, cars, other taxis, motorbikes and bicycles carrying entire families, rickshaws, pedestrians, cows, goats, slouching dogs, sleeping dogs and one tall, well-built, brown man with matted hair and beard—fully naked.

Yet even in the sparse rural traffic, our driver managed to swerve from side to side on the narrow road, seeming to play chicken with trucks, which were festooned with marigolds and swaying gold spangles to ward off disasters. In the aftermath of one of these adrenalin-charged encounters, I was blessed with an insight that proved as solid as faith. I promptly shared it with Stephanie.

It's okay. He's not going to crash. This taxi is all he has to make a living. He's not going to trash his capital.

In this peace of mind we floated from side to side as the taxi careened around the hairpin turns of the ghats. When the driver stopped near a small knot of Indians looking over the edge of a precipice, some of them approached our window. They spoke to us in excited tones, gesticulating toward the edge of the road. But all in Hindi or Marathi— only the gestures were clear.

Our driver explained, *A car fall down. They want you go look.*

Perhaps because we'd already been traveling for days, perhaps fatigue challenged our ability to summon that next depth of faith, perhaps because such a scene could break the spell of our peace of mind, perhaps because we were hungry and needed lunch, we shook our heads. We declined.

Well that had been in mid-June—so far so good—our first long journey together, Stephanie and I, in fifteen years. Then it had been a five-month camping trip all around the West, which had been wonderful. And terrible. And some things remained unresolved between us to that day.

By the time we were preparing to leave India, we were testy, barely speaking to each other, egos bruised, emotions raw and fluctuating. The thought of an eight-hour ride on Indian potholed roads with a sullen daughter was daunting. I believe we both welcomed Gayle's plea to join us. And Gayle was relieved to travel in what she regarded as safety in the company of India-experienced American women. She was upbeat, and her high energy was sufficient to diffuse the tension between Stephanie and me.

Still, I worried about the drive. We'd heard of flat tires, of mechanical problems, washed out roads, and my body and soul were too tenderized after a two-month stay near Meher Baba's tomb to bear further trials.

Our plan was to stop in Poona for lunch, then hire another taxi for the trip to Bombay. We stashed our luggage at a hotel, had a satisfying lunch at their restaurant, and returned to the reception counter. The clerk had arranged for a taxi and driver for us, all ready to go. We stepped out and I saw the license plate of our taxi: 222. A rush of joy and relief lifted my spirits. *Yes, Baba!*

It *would* be okay. I felt my prayers had been answered. We would have a safe and uneventful journey. Stephanie and I would survive our difficulties. Gayle would arrive home safely.

The men stowed our bags in the trunk. I hopped into the front seat next to the driver, letting Stephanie and Gayle enjoy each other's company for the long drive to Bombay. Which they did. And I relaxed in peace as our driver skillfully steered and swerved and beeped and braked and sped us across the countryside, over the ghats and into the tangle of Bombay.

Danger!

Sushi, our little black cat, the nemesis of many a bird, was prowling in the back yard as I brushed our chinchilla hare, Wiggy, on the patio one day in spring. *Chp, chp, chp*. A mockingbird warned Sushi not to come any closer. *Chp, chp, chp*. Wiggy's ears shot up and forward. He hip-hopped quickly around the low wall, across the yard. When he reached Sushi, he sat, thumping his hind foot, warning his friend of danger. After all, he'd heard it straight from the bird. *Chp, chp, chp!*

Can You Meet Me?

From central Mexico, my daughter's voice on the phone--
...should be in Nogales around eight tonight,
can you meet me?
I hear her bravado, thin through feathered Mexican wires:

She should be in Nogales around eight tonight.
The young man she's set on is leaving tomorrow for Virginia.
I hear her bravado, thin through feathered Mexican wires--
I'm coming home to Tucson. I want to go with him.

The young man she's set on is leaving tomorrow for Virginia.
I tell her I'll be there at the border.
I'm coming home to Tucson. I want to go with him.
I think of the long bus trip past plateaus, over deserts.

I tell her I'll be there at the border.
Arrive in Nogales early, eager to see her.
I think of the long bus trip past plateaus, over deserts.
Peer through the twelve-foot chain link fence.

Arrive early in Nogales, eager to see her.
Stand waiting through the darkness of slow hours.
Peer through the twelve-foot chain link fence.
Hang on to her words—*can you meet me?*

Stand waiting through the darkness of slow hours.
Trust that I heard her words right through Mexican wires.
Hang on to her words—*can you meet me?*
Distant shops crumple closed for the night.

Did I hear her words right through Mexican wires?
Scary stories foam up like uncaught lies.
Distant shops crumple closed for the night.
I beam desperate pleas through the chain link fence.

Scary stories foam up like uncaught lies.
It's after ten—the night beginning to swing shut.
I beam desperate pleas through the chain link fence.
Pray—where is she? What to do? *What?*

It's after ten—the night beginning to swing shut.
Images of her stranded or lost beat their wings inside me.
Pray—where is she? What to do? *What?*
Turn the key, please, God—let me see her face, familiar as rain.

Images of her stranded or lost beat their wings inside me.
Did I really hear what she said? Or did I dream....
Turn the key, please, God—let me see her face, familiar as rain.
Let her come walking toward me, a mirage of relief.

Did I really hear what she said? Or did I dream....
My daughter's voice on the phone—
Her bravado, thin through feathered Mexican wires—
Can you meet me?

A Scrabble Affair

I was visiting my friend, Marti, in London, Ontario, with our respective husbands, five-year-old daughters and two-year-old sons, when I saw my first Scrabble board there in 1971. It was passion at first sight. My nerve ends lit up, my brain fibers did Irish jigs with Balkan footwork. I had to have one of my own.

I splurged on a Scrabble set as soon as my mother-of-two-small-children-budget made it possible. My husband, Cliff, while less enamored, was game, and played stalwartly, losing ten games, winning one. He had an admirable attitude, saying he was learning from me and feeling very good when he beat me.

Wordplay was my element—beyond any duck-to-the-water cliché—it was the air I breathed. My brain reveled in putting letter tiles together in myriad ways, mix and match in endless algorithmic combinations. It was like eating Hagen-Dasz chocolate ice cream before there even was such a thing. Like eating Mom's strawberry shortcake with vanilla whipped cream. Fulfilling. Sublime.

Cliff and I played by the official rules, until he decided to divorce me. I don't think my excess of winning and his excess of losing was a salient factor in his decision. What he didn't know was that I was already determined to divorce him as soon as our son was in kindergarten. Are there rules about this?

When I met Donald in Greece summer of 1975, we camped all around the Peleponnesus, and played Scrabble every day. He'd played it with his third wife, Kathy, as they camped through

Europe and North Africa on their way to India. When Kathy left him in Marrakesh and returned to the USA with daughter, Pagan, two, I suspect her decision had little to do with how they played Scrabble.

Donald introduced variations to the game: whoever had three tiles of the same letter could show them and toss back one or two and redraw letters without penalty. Made sense. Who wants three i's or u's? Donald won more often than I did, but I didn't mind—I loved to play. Besides, he'd worked as editor of a dictionary, and being twenty years older, he should know more than me.

When Donald showed up in Michigan in the fall of 1976, we picked upon our Scrabble games again, with a new variation: we could substitute an appropriately lettered tile for a blank already played on the board, and replay the blank in a new capacity. That added some spice. Friend, Norm, not into words, but appreciative of passionate pastimes, gifted me with a deluxe Scrabble turntable set as a farewell gesture as Donald, my daughter, Stephanie and I set out in a poptop VW camper to explore the USA for the next five months. No one minded that it took up a chunk of space in the camper, which now held all I owned.

We played almost every day, sometimes twice, Donald and me, Stephanie, eleven, and me. Better than TV, which I never missed. We ended up in Venice Beach, California, and continued to play. After some months, Donald's daughter, Pagan, seven, came to live with us, and some months after that, Stephanie went to live with her father and brother, stepmother and half-sister in Illinois.

Donald's asthma turned into emphysema. We should return to the original rules, he said, except for the one about of three of a kind, in case this way of playing should interfere when we played with others. So we did that until he lost interest in playing, finding the effort to breathe a fulltime endeavor. He died on the first day of spring in 1980, and I am certain that changing the rules of Scrabble back and forth had absolutely nothing to do with that.

The following year I spent some months in India at the Pilgrim Center of Meher Baba. Among the games available in the dining hall was—yes! a Scrabble set. A partner showed up in Christine, the resident nurse from Adelaide , Australia. She won the first game we played--then, though we played almost daily, sometimes twice, she never won another game. After we left India for our respective continents in March, we exchanged a letter or two, but I never saw her again. Nor has anyone I spoke to heard from her in the years since. I am almost positive that my obsessive winning and her valiant losing had nothing to do with that.

In the fall of 1981, Kathy invited me to live with them in Norfolk, Virginia. and home school Pagan for sixth grade. Kathy had come to Venice to settle Donald's affairs after he'd died, and she and Pagan and I had gotten on well. No surprise that Kathy was a whiz at "bingos," seven-letter words for a fifty-point bonus. I had better luck playing with Pagan, eleven by this time. We adhered to the three of a kind rule and the exchangeable blank as well.

At the beginning of 1983 I arrived in Tucson, having agreed to marry Karl. We had met through our mutual friend, Norm, in Detroit, and Karl had visited me in Norfolk. Twice. The second visit led to a proposal, an acceptance, then mutual shock at what we'd just agreed to. Karl cleared out of the Detroit area and ended up in sunny Tucson. I remembered it well from my camping tour and wholeheartedly said "yes." I found a travel Scrabble set at a supermarket and presented it for Karl's approval. He was game, said he was good speller, having won his eighth grade spelling bee and a dictionary. I, in fact, had done likewise. His dictionary came in handy since I always advocated for playing "open dictionary" style, and not bother with challenging each other's words.

The first time Karl and I played, I won and he was disgruntled— a Scorpio-- not a good loser. I pointed out the idea of his picking up skills as we played. The second time, Karl was losing again— he tipped the board, jumbling the tiles. I'd never seen such a thing. The third time we tried, I had a bingo and Karl said he didn't want to play anymore. We never played again.

Looking for players, I found a Scrabble club, which led to a Scrabble tournament. I came in second, but beat the winner, a man from Phoenix, so I declared myself the Scrabble champ of Tucson for 1986. Scrabble took a back seat during the years I studied for a master's degree in counseling at the U of A. I went to one more tournament, and ran into the Phoenix man I'd beat. He upbraided me for not playing more tournaments, I shrugged--grad school was more important now.

I did not enjoy playing in that tournament. It was not fun. I decided that Scrabble in my life had to be fun—so no more tournaments. While I know all the two-letter words and most of the three-letter words, I refuse to memorize lists, as some players do—even the four-letter words. Ugh. I have the lists and refer to them as well as to my official Scrabble dictionary, but it is all for my enjoyment.

Now I play by myself, right hand versus left hand. I play cooperatively, not cutthroat. I keep the three of a kind rule, the exchangeable blank rule and one other that suits me. When I play with others, I stick to the accepted rules, but my suggestion of open dictionary and the three of a kind rule are usually welcome.

In our thirtysome years of marriage, Karl and I've had the usual challenges, surprises, disappointments in each other, and the lack of Scrabble playing between us surely was one of them for me. At the same time, Karl and I agree that this absence of Scrabble games has not had one whit of adverse affect on our abiding love for each other.

Not Too Soon

Morning sun casts
shadows, accents
ridges, canyons:
the Catalinas
brood ahead,
not multiplying.

Muscled young men crawl
booted over wood
frames of incipient town houses,
pound nails to the brawny
boom of a current
Boss on the airwaves.

A hotpink-
haltered blonde rumbles
past in a camouflage jeep,
blares her own hot punk beat.

Glued under the sun's glare
by noon,
the Catalinas will be one
undifferentiated mass,
like this latest
subdivision.
Soon.

I keep walking,
turn west.

Mom: A Requiem in Retrospect

She'd complain about how much work it was, the garden—hauling of manure, digging it in—Dad did most of that. Planting seeds of string and wax beans, leaf lettuce, parsley, dill, cucumbers, carrots, and sets of onions, garlic, tomatoes, winter cabbages for sauerkraut and kohlrabi—a litany of goodness—they shared all that, worked together. As for the fruits, Dad fussed over his peach trees, Mom over her Barlett pears, her strawberry patch, the huckleberry and raspberry canes. Weeding, watering, dusting for bugs. My job was to pick off the horrifying, fat green tomato caterpillars, pick strawberries every day after school in the month of June, pick beans, pull onions, carrots, lettuce, parsley and dill as she needed them for cooking. I'd complain about it too, but she was a good cook and we ate well, and we didn't complain about that.

But the flower garden was her very own. Its blossoms' sensuous colorfest touched her tenderest part, the part still young, innocent—still untrampled, uncompromised. They soothed and reflected uncomplicated, sweet-scented love. No one to mock her heart's longing, to scorn her village accent. No one to turn on her, ferocious with thorny questions. Peonies and tulips required only earthy elements, sun and rain—these she could promise without fear of marauding hands beyond her control. Here God kissed her eyes as she arranged the radiant reds of salvias, the golden yellows and purples of dahlias, the velveted blues and violets of pansies and irises, the glorious whites and many hues of the stately gladioli. She orchestrated the heights, breadths and textures, the very shape of the air between petals. She reigned in adoration over every stained glass patch and row. Just so.

Mom loved most purely through these flowers she nurtured: daisies, peonies, marigolds, sweet alyssum, asters. By her hands they were sown, fed, watered, allotted shade and sun. Their slender green stalks struggled through the dark loam, took heart, budded and burst into profuse blooms, each a sunsmile in her heart. They had no resentment, no reason to fear sudden heavy hands. Their names, *Margaretenblumen, Stiefmütterchen* (little stepmothers), were safe in her mouth.

All her life she'd wanted to be loved. Comforted. Her mother was self-centered, her father needy, siblings contentious. Dad fell short too—I won't go into that here. My older sister became her confidante, her guide even, in the English-speaking world. I loved her wholeheartedly, until she beat me when I was six, for something I didn't do— I kept my distance from that day on. She turned to lovers, she turned to food, to doctors and drugs, one handful of which finally led to her no rosy death.

For the three decades since, I have cried and weeded out the abandonment, the harsh hands, brutal threats and demands, the lies, so her love as shown to those magnificent flowers can stand clear and shine. And I, no gardener, just manage to keep most things in the yard alive—I long for blooms. Roses. I tend a small garden of roses.

Role Model

About ten years ago I attended a workshop in Las Vegas on how to work with battered women and men. It was led by Noel Larson, from St. Paul, MN, who, along with her husband, also gave trainings in the Crucible Model of couples therapy, as developed by David Schnarch, the genius psychiatrist. I was so impressed with Noel that I later called her from Tucson, and asked if she would be my phone therapist. She agreed.

For an hour every other week I unloaded heart and mind of puzzles and conundrums that troubled me. There was one thing in particular, of a very intimate nature, that I had been trying to accomplish, something highly advocated by David Schnarch. When I brought up this elusive challenge, Noel gave a small, light laugh, and said, *Oh we all want to be able to do that.*

Her words were music to my ears, but her tone was pure balm. In this one sentence, given in such an accepting, acknowledging tone, she gave me permission to lay to rest years and bushels of worry of inadequacy. Although Noel was two months younger than me, she embodied the voice of a mother I never had, the voice of understanding and complete acceptance. This is something I have also been grateful to experience throughout my years of being in these writing groups.

Muscles of mind and body relaxed. A lifetime of tension dissolved. I felt allowed to be myself, to like myself and simply do my best. I learned to offer the people I spend time with my best heartfelt approximation of Noel's tone. It is what so many of us long for—understanding and acceptance.

The Telephone Call -- 2000

I was sitting in the middle of my fifth grade classroom, while the teacher took the class through a creative writing exercise. I so wanted him to call on me and hear my very good idea. It came to me clearly, then and there--I was going to be a writer. I finally took my first fiction writing class at Pima Community College, West Campus, in the fall of 1999. I was in my mid-fifties and very excited to be in a class of writers.

The instructor and my classmates at Pima gave me critical and helpful comments through the semester. We were encouraged to submit our short stories to the Martindale Literary Contest, which my friend, Nancy had long been involved with. I submitted my final class project, *The Human Touch: A Triptych*. The judge would be an unidentified, out-of-town author.

I was admitted into the Advanced Fiction class for the spring semester. These writers had teeth, and occasionally, claws. Some were gifted. I felt I had to work hard to measure up, and rarely felt I did. I struggled through, learning, learning.

One afternoon in mid-May my phone rang. It was Nancy. *Are you sitting down?* she said.

Immediately I wondered--had someone in the Meher Baba community died? *Okay, I'm sitting. News from India?*

No-o, she said. *I'm calling to let you know--you won the Martindale!*

Shock made me rise from the dining room chair. My eyes searched for confirmation in mesquite branches out front, in the Catalina Mountains--still there, north of Tucson. Skies still blue above them. All this fused with hearing, seeing, feeling the smiles and delight in Nancy's voice. But I remained speechless.

You can't tell anyone though, Nancy said. *Well, you can tell Karl. So then it will be a surprise at the opening night of the Pima Writers Conference at the end of May.*

I have no memory of what I said. Consumed with searching for how to *be* when a dream has come true.

Dark Horse

After the last fiction class they invited me to tag along to Molloy's for drinks--the clique that had ignored me all semester. The buzz around the table was all about who'd win the Literary Award. *Stacy will get first place,* Rheta said. *Lou will get second, and I'll get third.* I listened and remembered raising my bedroom blind before dawn some weeks before—seeing the long arc of a meteor flashing south. Remembered the stark dream in which I raced against the bigger, faster ones and *knew* I'd win. From the edge of the circle I said, *I'll be the dark horse.* They didn't even look at me. But they looked at Rheta when she said, *I'll be the dark horse.* On the evening of the Award presentation, I saw empty seats at their table. *So sorry,* they said, *we're saving them.* In my new outfit I sat with Karl and friend, Judith, near the clique's table. *They're still buzzing,* I said, *about who'll win first place.*

VILLAGE AVENUE, TUCSON

Making a List

Our tenant would receive her PhD from the University of Arizona in May, 2004, and return with her son and mother to Taiwan. Karl and I knew we did not want to go on being landlords. We'd bought this duplex in 1999 so his father could be close to us as he slowly succumbed to lung cancer. In January, 2004 we made a list. After twentysome years in Tucson, we had a clear idea of what we wanted in a house.

Rita, our real estate agent, wrote down what we wanted: three bedrooms, one of which could be used as an office for my therapy practice; two bathrooms, one of which would be accessible by clients; wood floors; both swamp cooling and central air conditioning; a carport or garage that could be transformed into a music studio for Karl; an appropriate place in the living room to hang a very large photograph of Meher Baba; another appropriate place to hang a horizontal scroll of artwork by our daughter, Stephanie; easy access to nature, where I could walk every day, a safe yard for our two cats; a Jacuzzi.

Then there was the No list: no new houses, no tract housing, no adjacent major thoroughfares, no Home Owners Associations, no seeing someone's wall as I look out a window, no wall-to-wall carpeting.

Karl and I agreed on what we thought we could afford.

For three days of the first week Rita took me to see three or four houses a day. *These are just to rule things out,* she said, and pointed out attractive features in each place, like higher countertops in rebuilt kitchens because women are taller now. At the end of the second week I took Karl to see three of the houses Rita had shown me. Two were "almosts." One was intriguing, but already spoken for.

As a week went by with no houses, I felt despondent of ever finding exactly what we wanted.

Rita was also selling our duplex, showing it in Open House mode on a few Sundays. It was delicate, having to ask our tenant friends to vacate their home for several hours on a Sunday. That part of the duplex was a normal two bedroom house, with an Arizona room connecting to our house. Our part included an enclosed carport and breezeway, full of skylights, massive beams and a large ficus tree growing out of a space in the brick floor—all of which had the effect of a cathedral. Also a Jacuzzi which didn't work.

It was a unique property. We hoped someone would want it as much as we had five years earlier. People came and exclaimed over built in shelves and cupboards in the living room, the greenhouse windows in the living and dining rooms, that gave excellent views of the Catalinas, the sense of space with the kitchen open to the dining and living areas. Some expressed interest, but no one made an offer.

Early in February Rita took me to see three morehouses. We must have seen the one on Village last because I can't think of any reason to have looked at another after that one. It sat up on a small ridge behind a half acre of desert growth. LJ, the owner, was sitting at a small table by a fountain out front. She had an accent, which I guessed to be Slavic, and I asked—yes—Yugoslavian. Serbian or Croatian? I don't remember her response, but we had good eye contact and began to connect.

First, she said, *I show you this*, and she led us up a path into virgin desert, forty acres of it—the horse and hiking trails of WestwardLook Resort. *Here I walk every day.*

Easy access to nature—check.

Walking back to the territorial-style house, I noted adobe brick walls, a stately pine out front. Trying to keep hope in line, I stepped through the front doorway into a wide ceramic tiled hall that led to sliding doors looking onto the backyard. Yes. Living and dining rooms to the right, all in one—wood floors, beamed ceilings, three large arched windows looked out on a gravel drive and a front yard of virgin desert. No neighbors in sight. Yes, yes, yes.

My heart had begun to hum.

Arched doorway into the kitchen—solid oak cupboards everywhere, copper hood for the range, window looking out on the Catalinas and a pool inside a walled backyard. Next to the kitchen, a family room with a beehive fireplace and sliding doors to the backyard. So far, so very good.

Down a narrower hall, a small full bath on the right, a small bedroom on the left, and at the end of the hall, a spacious master bedroom with a small three-quarter bath, sliding doors to the backyard, and a medium sized bedroom on the left, looking out front. Perfect.

LJ and Rita were talking, talking. The house was built in 1971 for a friend of Howard Hughes. The kitchen had been remodeled. They'd added tile-roofed porticos along the east, south and west sides of the house. Swamp cooler and central AC. I probably said some nice things, asked questions, but mostly I was all eyes. All eyes, taking in the possibilities, my mind buzzing, seeing where to put things. Yes, wall space enough for Baba's photograph and Stephanie's print work. Yes, a room for an office at one end of the house—we could replace one window with a door, add an overhang. There was plenty of room for several cars to park. Yes, yes, yes.

She led us through a portico to the drive-through carport with an attached laundry room. To become Karl's studio—check. Citrus trees in the back, orange, lemon, grapefruit. Washes both north and south, and desert outside the backyard walls. A whole second yard adjacent on the north for their friendly pitbull, to become our catyard. I had no qualms about substituting the pool for a Jacuzzi.

They were asking $17,000 more than we had agreed on.

I found our house, I told Karl, giving him just a small preview, not wanting to spoil the delight of seeing it all for himself. But when he saw it, he complained that the wrought iron screens on the sliding doors would make the house dark, that there was no place for his studio, that it was more than we wanted to spend. Dumbfounded, I pointed out the obvious. He went to look at it again, to see it without my troublesome enthusiasm shadowing him, but he continued to grumble.

A house like this would not be on the market long. I showed Karl the list we'd made, asked if I was missing something. I realized, sadly, that if he wasn't on board for this house, I would have to let it go.

It was time he needed, to process the house, the price—his process often being different from mine. After a few days he said, *Okay, if the house payment is under $__, we can make an offer.* It was. Stretching our budget, we offered $2,000 less than their asking price. They accepted.

In the meantime we had three offers to buy our duplex. We accepted the one from a Tucson woman over the one from an East coast investor.

I had never fantasized about "my dream house." Years ago I had the thought that I was neither interested nor any good at planning an ideal home. I figured someday I would find a place that someone else had put a lot of thought into, that also suited me. I could add cosmetic touches, like having it painted. For this house we did more than that, making the changes necessary for office and studio, changing all the outdoor lighting, adding fencing to keep our cats safe.

After we'd all signed all the papers, and the house was ours, I asked LJ if they'd had other offers. *Oh yes,* she said, *but we just decided to go with you.* Was it the good eye contact and knowing something about Yugoslavia? Or was it a God thing?

The Cat, the Rat and the Table: A Fable

The Set-up

I was up before sunrise in the first week of June, soon after we'd moved into our beautiful new home just north of Tucson. I'd fed Max, fetched the paper, putzed in the kitchen, made tea and carried it into the living room. About to sit down with the Sunday paper, I was surprised to hear Karl shuffling in the hall this early. I was still standing when he appeared barefoot at the archway that opens into the living room. Just then Max trotted in carrying a kangaroo rat in his mouth. He stopped between us.

"Out, out," Karl and I intoned in unison.

That worked with Minnie, Max's sister—she'd know to take her toothsome treasure outside and eat it there without our interference. But Max, bless his kitty heart, always got confused—he dropped the rat.

The rat ran under the loveseat. We moved the loveseat and the rat ran under an endtable. Karl removed the lamp from the table, lifted it and set it on its side in the center of the room. Now the rat had run into the center of a rolled-up runner. (We were clearly not completely settled in and various items were still in flux.) Karl deftly unrolled the carpet, trying to keep his bare feet out of the rat's most likely next trajectory. The rat ran to a leg of the table and stuck itself into the little triangular space where the leg joins the tabletop.

The Backstory

We'd bought that square, oak veneer endtable seventeen years ago, along with a sofa and a loveseat, when we moved into the Ellis Street house. At the end of twelve years there, the table had broken down some, but since we needed more furniture for the larger Third Street house, Karl patched it together. It sat next to the carport door in Karl's studio, holding drawers of video tapes and a large, wooden rajah puppet. As we sorted things this spring in preparation for the move (the last one, I hope!) to the Village Avenue house—what to sell, what to give away, what to discard—I asked Karl about this table.

"I want it for my studio," he said.
"Fine."

We were enclosing a drive-through carport to become Karl's studio at the Village house. As it often happens, the construction was not complete by our moving date. This meant that stacks and stacks of boxes had to be stored in the house, along with the old sofa and loveseat, his recording equipment, computers and various other furnishings, including this endtable. The house was so crowded that the piano and some other things had to sit outside under the portico for a week, until the studio was ready, carpet and all. For two days we wedged a walkway through the living room, then Karl moved things around a bit so we could sit comfortably. He put this endtable in a corner and set a handsome brass lamp on it.

A week later, on a Friday, he had a couple of movers put all his gear and furnishings into his new studio. They worked hard for two hours. Karl said to me, "Look around—is there anything else that belongs in the studio."

"This table," I said, indicating the one in the corner.
"No," he said. "I like that table there."
"Well, I have other tables to go there," I said.
"This table is just right here, with the big brass lamp on it."
"The only reason we kept that table is that you wanted it for your studio."
"But now I like it here," he said.

Clear I didn't want that table in the living room, I gave up for the moment.

The Outcome

So, it was Sunday morning and there was a kangaroo rat stuck in the underneath corner of the table. I didn't say a word. Nor did Karl. He picked up the table and set it outside the front door. I promptly moved a handsome old, refinished, solid oak round table into the empty corner, and set the lamp on it.

"I want this table to stay here." I said.
Karl didn't have anything to say to that.

We settled down to read the paper, drink our tea. I went out a couple of times to look at the rat, its tail and one paw hanging out of the little triangle. Had we injured the poor thing? I thought not. Eventually Karl went out, picked up the table and gave it a whack. The rat dropped out and scuttled off into our desert front yard.

"I guess I'll take this table to the studio," he said.
"Okay."

Epilogue

The cat, Max, continues to be a sweet, sometimes befuddled, but excellent ratter. The rat, as far as we know, we never saw again.

Over the following weeks, we arranged and rearranged things in Karl's studio. He repeatedly lamented he had too much stuff, yet was not ready to let much of it go. We did ship an ancient Victrola and a rocking chair to his cousin. We set up shelves all along one wall and he filled them with boxes and boxes. Still, there was too much stuff. One day he sighed and said, "I don't think there'll ever be room for this (yes, that) table in the studio."

It was too big to fit into either of our cars, so it sat on the back patio for a while, until the man who did some fencing for us hauled it away in his pick-up.

The Moral

      Pshaw—none.

The Question—the Burning Question

Now, who orchestrated this? That Karl and Max and the rat converged at the same moment? That the rat ran up the leg of that table and stayed there? *Who?*

Desert Walk

Narrow trail, cactus edged—
a cardinal flames,
settles on mesquite before me

flies out of sight—
and again
my steps erase
tracks of quail,
coyotes on the path,

even remnants
of my own footprints.

This New Life

I break a glass jar, a nailfile.
I spill salad on the floor—
it's going to cost me something,
this new life heading my way,

this door I'm about to slip through.

It's already been settled—
Signed and agreed to
in my heart of hearts.

Now to just watch--
what torn away,
what unfolding?

Stephanie

When she was a long-legged
eleven, she climbed door jambs,
grinned spread-eagled,
Mom, look at me!
from the kitchen doorway.

Now her eyes mirror a riot
of morning glories. Tawny-
red curls tangle in tendrils
not of her making.

She looks like she grew up
in a garden,
walled but ungated,
shaded by elms.

Like an unspoken prayer,
a silver heart locket
nestles below her throat.

~~~~~~~~~~~~~~~

you leave—the quiet
settles in—silence thickens
space where you are not

Plantings

A part of me hopes to be planted here in this house. That I will be able to live here for the rest of my life, enjoying the Catalina Mountains, the desert views and sunsets, the desert walks. It's occurred to me that I have walked toward this place all my life. And here I am.

I've told Karl I want my body to be cremated, and if we're still here, my ashes to be strewn, dug in among the rose bushes. Planted. Meff told me once that the rose is the only flower that knows it is beautiful. My ashes would nourish that beauty.

My spirit, on the other hand, has been led toward Meher Baba, probably from the beginning of my soul drop existence. I must have seen Him with my eyes in my last life in order to have experienced His Presence in this life. An experience which planted me heart and soul in Him.

I travel from this house to Bisbee, to Phoenix, Telluride, Myrtle Beach, India–and I'm always happy to come home. In a similar way, I take excursions into the material, gross world—buy alpaca sweaters, eat chocolate and ice cream, pay bills, get mad at Karl or envious of someone—but sooner or later I remember my best self and return to the roots, the grounding of love, of truth, of beauty.

The Occasional Cup.

On rainy mornings
and slow afternoons
I dream of tea laced with cream,
and indulge once a month or so
willing to pay what it exacts—
two days of torpor and fatigue.

Years ago I threw coffee into the dhuni,
the saintly fire that consumes desire.
Coffee no longer tempts me
but tea I will not throw in,
preferring to indulge in nostalgia
laced with longing
for that brief and bracing comfort,

not willing to let go
of wanting--
a small grief
but one nonetheless--

a grief I will not yet end.

~~~~~~~~~~~

For someone who does
not love life all that much,
I sure do love to dance.

Winners and Losers

"Elizabeth's tenant found four kittens on his roof. Thinks their mother is dead."

"Yeah?"
"Three of them are black."
"And we collect black cats."

"Haven't you been wanting one that'll be especially yours? Lie in your lap—not just mine all the time. Not scared of men."

"Sure. What, you think we should get a kitten?"
"Could."
"What about Minnie and Max?"
"Yeah, that's the question. Will they accept a new kitten?"
"If we got two they'd feel more comfortable together in a new place."

Saturday, Elizabeth took us to Mike's place. His Chow nosed us in after Mike vouched for us. One black kitten was already spoken for. So two black and one Siamese, little, six weeks old, cute as could be expected. We held them. They let us. We petted them. They let us. We tried to see—girls or boys—they squirmed and mewed, and we didn't really know enough to tell at this age.

"I'm thinking to keep the Siamese," Mike said.
"Whaddya think?" Karl asked me.
"Up to you."
"Okay. We'll take the two black ones. There's just one thing...."

He explained the Minnie and Max clause. Mike set the kittens on top of his table, all together one last time. The Chow watched their every move—his babies too. The Siamese was alpha cat already, chased the others, wrestled them around. Who would he boss now, the Chow?

They were quiet as mice on the long ride home, just one little mew between them. I went in the house first, made sure Minnie was in our bedroom, scooped Max off the sofa and deposited him next to her. Closed the door.

Karl slid the cat carrier under my desk in the den. The babies were piled in a back corner. I spooned chicken catfood into the dish I bought for them, set it near the carrier, opened the door. One crept forward, cautious, sniffing, sniffing....bounced out and stuck its face into the dish. In less than a minute, the other followed. Once they'd licked the bowl clean, they explored the den.

I made tea, set out cookies and chips. We read, watched the babies bounce and scramble for close to an hour. A homey scene.

"Time for Max," I said. I got the kittens safely into the carrier. Brought Max out, and set about brushing and combing him, all of which he enjoyed until he heard a rustle from the carrier. He looked, bewildered. Stepped closer, sniffed. Jerked back and positively slunk out the catdoor. Sat outside the glass door and looked in. Ears forward, bewildered.

"Not too bad for a first encounter," I said. Karl agreed.

Now Minnie. She got a bit closer to the carrier than Max did, maybe said something under her catbreath, because one of the kittens hissed. Minnie hissed back and freaked: back to the bedroom, behind our bed, her ultimate hidey place.

"Okay, not too bad for a first time," I said. Karl agreed.

M&M slunk around all evening, gave the kittens in the carrier a wide berth, cast sideways glances in all directions, not knowing whence the next abomination might appear. The kittens slept piled in their corner, sometimes opening a shiny eye at us.
M&M did not eat their evening treats.

Sunday I was up before dawn. Mewmew, mewmew. I smelled that the babies had pottied on the towel in their carrier. I threw the towel out. Cleaned up the babies. Fed them, showed them once more where to go potty, scratched their paws in the kitty litter. Eventually it would register. One of them had already peed in the litter box last night.

Minnie stayed on our bed, curled next to Karl's feet. Didn't come out as usual for her breakfast. Max nowhere in sight. When I went out for the paper, I heard him mewing on the roof. Karl got him down. We didn't know how he got up there, so we didn't know how to stop him. He hadn't done that since we were gone for a week last summer, left them with the catsitter. Problem was—from the roof, he'd climb down the pine trunk into the front yard, where he was vulnerable to any passing bobcat or coyote. Max wouldn't eat either. No food, no water.

In the afternoon I saw Max out front. He came easily when I called him, zoomed in the front door. It wasn't exactly like he was running away from home, just that he took to the roof when he felt threatened, and then one thing led to another.

And that was the deal breaker.

We figured M&M would eventually eat again, drink again, even find way to coexist with the kittens. But if the presence of kittens drove Max to the roof—well, we spent five months and a sum of money, an amount we would never admit to—to fence the back yards so M&M could not get out, nor could coyotes, bobcats or snakes get in. Just couldn't have Max that freaked.

"Hey Mike, it isn't going to work out here. I'm gonna have to bring the kittens back." Karl explained about the roof and the coyotes. "Yeah, it's too bad."

Karl scooped the kittens back in with their Siamese brother, who had mewed for them terribly after we'd taken them away. They romped and rolled—hello, hello. The Chow smiled, pleased.

I was resigned. It would have been me feeding the little ones, cleaning them up. Only Karl was very sad. Thought we'd care for these little guys for the rest of their lives.

Monday morning Max was out front again. He came in when Karl went for the paper. M&M sniffed, sniffed around the den, heard no kitten mews. They stopped slinking, stretched out on the rugs and sofas again. Showed up for breakfast, demanded their treats.

Fireworks

The first time was on a friend's sailboat
on Chesapeake Bay as we sat spooning
in the July heat. *Is this for real, you and me?*
My back cushioned
against your chest. So solid.
Our hands, palm to palm, so familiar.
Our summer skin lit by the blaze
and spray of fireworks.
We breathed our delight in unison.
Reds, whites and electric blues
presided over the night sky—
skittering in all directions.
Mandalas of flash and flame,
they'd fade and fall.
Would we?

How many fireworks have we thrilled to
over this quarter century together?
(How many have we created and survived?)

Last night we lay quiet
in the last three minutes of the year.
Suddenly--Bang! Flash!
Fireworks burst and spangled the new year sky.
Reds, greens and yellows shot up
from the resort behind us.
Side by side we watched the sizzling show,
not spooning. Still familiar.
Still delighted.

Nudes

1

I lie belly down on a white wicker sofa in a white room.
Face turned away from the eye of the camera.
Light from three windows drifts
along my shoulder and back, buttock and thigh.
I am a still life. Frozen in soft white.

2

My father, on his back, unseeing, in a hospital bed.
They've taken his false teeth. Mouth wide open, gasping.
Strands of his hair, finally silver, strewn on the pillow.
His hand, still big as a baseball mitt, closes over mine,
grasps me like a straw, convulses every other moment—
pain (he'd caused us) finally alive in him.

3

Kathleen's body laid out on a tall table, under a white sheet.
She didn't want a viewing, but as her nephew, Karl got us in.
Face a wax mask.
Don't look, I feel her say. Don't look at me like this.
We say a small prayer and scram like naughty children.

4

I don't go to see Mom lying on the front seat
of her Ford Galaxy still in the garage.
I don't go in to see her at the funeral home.
Stay in the airless cubicle, wait for Dad and Ilse.
On their faces—reflections of her despair, self-pity—
what I try to shun.

5
Donald on the middle of the floor,
covered with a sheet. Bet he hates that. Sense
his subtle body hovering, watching.
Uncover his face—waxen grimace.
Beetle casing sloughed off.
Last three minutes alone with him, I fish
the twenties I'd given him out of his pockets.
He'd understand.

6
Alex comes to me in an astral dream,
bleeding,
bones jutting through broken skin.
Anguish floods my veins.
But his face—shining at me.
It's okay, Mom. I did good,
written all over his luminescence.

7
I long
to see You seeing me,
as only You can—
with that absolute recognition
that tells me
I am Yours
in and out of time.
See You see through me, into me
and beyond—
to Me.

8
Every joy, every gain
every ache and pain
is a drop of rain
by the grace
of Your Name.

9
For my birthday Karl plays and sings
the Beatles' "64" song,
changes the words to fit him and me.
He comes to "I couldn't love you more,"
and I hear his heart naked in his chest,
like a Catholic Jesus, but not bleeding.
Just beating in lovetime.

Walking

The path stony here,
sandy there—always footprints
steady before me.

What She Will Take

She will take her clothes and personal things—that goes without saying. She will take her paintings, prints and drawings. Her paints, pencils, brushes, paper, drawing board. She will take all her books and photographs of Meher Baba. She will leave the sofa his parents bought—*I'd wanted one big enough for both of us to stretch out on.* Take the full spectrum lamp and the wok we'd sent. Leave the bed and the goosedown quilt—*it has a lot of history,* she said. She will take her computer, having erased all the movies and CDs she'd asked him to please not record. She'll take Nixie, her little black cat, who has travelled with her from Tucson to Champaign to Seattle, from apartment to apartment to that house. She will leave that house—*I don't care about it—he'll probably sell it.* She will leave his anxiety and anger, but take some sadness—*I still love him, but it feels like I'm in prison.* She will take her Hyundai station wagon that we helped her to buy, but definitely leave the Taurus wagon his parents sent him. She will take the key to her new apartment, the one with the miniature Statue of Liberty across the street. She will leave him a letter.

She Tells Me

She's surrounded by boxes, mainly of books.
She's looking in catalogs for bamboo mats
to protect the carpet under her new drafting
table from paint splatters. She's ordered
a Japanese screen to shelter works in progress
when friends are over. She is hungry for beef
with tangy maple dip at a favorite restaurant.

> I don't tell my daughter how we ate shepherd's pie
> in front of the fireplace, shared tales from our respective
> days. I don't tell her the recipe—half made up,
> half remembered—so homey, so filling.

She's had an email from her husband:
How are you? I'm alright, she wrote back,
but I'm not ready to talk to you.
She misses him, but doesn't tell him
where she's moved to.

> I don't tell her the fire was merry,
> spontaneous with licks and sparks,
> that our cats stayed in the den with us,
> ate supper when we did, as a family.

Her little black cat, Nixie plays again
as she did as a kitten, sleeps safely now
on the new chair, out in the open.

> I don't tell her how we kiss goodnight,
> face to face—wordless—touching palm to palm,
> fingers interlaced, infused with gratitude
> for her loss, her gain, her courageous break.

She's bought herself a new queen-sized bed
and a futon sofa for when we come to visit.

> I don't tell her I never
> wanted her to marry him.

Quietude

Sun descending
to the western horizon,
brilliant white
saturates the room,
lampshade profile
sharpens on the wall,
spider plant leaves
spray graceful shadows,
a stark silhouette
stalks a carved coyote.

I savor a great need for emptiness.

Sun embraces the horizon,
light softens to cream,
shadows mellow,
cream thickens to buttercup,
gleams amber,
ripens to apricot,
blooms rosy,
deepens to fierce marigold--
outlines seep slowly
into the light,
afterglow pales
across the wall,
and fades.

Young Raccoon

hobbles along
the Myrtle Beach trail
falls over on its side
struggles up--
takes three steps
falls again,
three steps and falls,
(we follow quietly)
and again
takes slow steps
down a shallow bank
      drinks at the brook
      falls over.

Next morning
a still form
under
fallen leaves.

We depart in silence.

This Path

I walk this path,
stony or sandy in turn,
choose right or left by whim—
a desire for sun or shade,
for shorter or longer route this time,
as in rounds of lifetimes—

the push of birth, a first tooth,
learning to tie shoelaces,
my own driver's license at last,
a job, a child, a mortgage,
the ache of greying joints--

and the moment of return,
that need for a great emptiness—

again I set out--
this curve,
this clump of cactus,
birdsong,
packrat nest,
shade of mesquite,
fragrance of desert rain,

this steep slope and slippery descent.

This path--always narrow,
still littered with what came before,
even my own footprints.

Fathom the Depth

A flash of black cat streaks across heavy traffic
headed right into a car—will he make it?
I slow to let a van pass—I have to know—
see a black bundle scrabbling to the curb, broken.

Headed right into a car—how to make it?
I'm in the furthest lane, traffic all around,
see the black bundle scrabbling to the curb, broken.
Half a block away, I scan the scope of what to do.

I'm in the furthest lane, traffic all around.
I know I won't go back to find that bundle.
One block and I still scan the scope of what to do.
Better it died outright—less pain for him, and me.

I know I won't go back to find that bundle.
Heartmind in outrage, demanding: why, God, why!
Better it died outright—less pain for him, and me.
On the CD, Jim Meyer sings of God: *You alone exist.*

Heartmind in outrage, demanding: why, God, why!
I hear the song: *You are the Ocean of Mercy*
on the CD, Jim singing: *You alone exist.*
This pain, this mercy, I cannot put together.

I hear the song: *You are the Ocean of Mercy.*
How to understand? Tears run hot for this black cat.
This pain, this mercy, I cannot put together.
You are the cat (and the wheel) *You alone exist.*

How to understand? I weep for this black cat.
But You are the cat, the curb, car and driver.
This pain, this mercy, try to come together.
Yes, You are the street, the traffic, pain and tears,

and You take all suffering upon Yourself.
You are all sorrows, all tears, shed and unshed.
This pain, this mercy begin to come together--
You are the cat, curb, wheel and driver, pain and tears.

You are all sorrows, all tears, shed and unshed.
It's beyond me to fathom the depth of all this:
You are the black bundle scrabbling to the curb.
black flash of cat streaking across the traffic.

Sometimes

life feels like a sentence,
with a period at the end
of a long saga,
a period of weightlessness,
devoid of daily needs or tasks—
no body to sustain or cater to—
mind still there,
but aloft and without care,
until the next capital
on the horizon
beginning
the next sentence—
dawning or looming.

Holy Water

It came in the mail in a plastic bottle that once held a Coca Cola water product, bubble-wrapped. Sent from a suburb of Detroit by Karl's Muslim friend, Majid. The water now in the bottle was by no means a Coca Cola product. Majid, on hajj to Mecca, drew this water from the Well of Zamzam.

According to the Book of Genesis, Abraham and Sarah were childless at the ages of eighty-five and seventy-six, respectively. She sent him her Egyptian handmaid, Hagar, to take as a second wife, but soon tasted the bitterness of this arrangement. Hagar fled. An Angel responded to her distress, told her she was with child, a son, that God would multiply her seed without number. With this message, she took heart and returned to Abraham, who named his son Ishmael, "God shall hear."

When Ishmael was thirteen, Sarah also bore a son, Isaac. Soon after she told Abraham that Hagar and her son must leave their household. Deeply grieved, Abraham took comfort when he heard God's promise that Ishmael would be blessed.

Hagar and Ishmael were guided to Becca, a barren valley in Arabia, "forty camel days south of Canaan." Here they became desperately thirsty, so that Hagar feared for her son's life. Ishmael cried out to God as his mother paced from rock to rock, and after her seventh passage sat to rest. Here an Angel appeared and gave her this message from God: "Fear not, for God hath heard the voice of the lad where he is." She opened her eyes to see a well of water.

By God's grace an abundant spring of pure water welled up from the sand at Ishmael's heel. The valley soon became a stopping place for caravans which gathered around the Well of Zamzam. Abraham visited his son in this holy place to which Hagar had been led. According to the Koran, God showed Abraham the exact place, adjacent to the Well of Zamzam, where and how he and Ishmael were to build a sanctuary, the Ka'bah, to house a celestial stone. God told Abraham to institute the rite of pilgrimage to Becca, or Mecca as it was called later. When Hagar told him how she had trod from rock to rock searching for help, he included these two rocks and the well in the rite—that pilgrims should pass seven times round the Ka'bah and seven times around these two rocks as well.

In time Mecca came under the control of Jurhumites from Yemen. They were toleratd by the descendants of Abraham since Ishmael's second wife was a kinswoman of Jurham. But when the Jurhumites committed too many injustices they were driven out. In revenge they filled the Well of Zamzam with treasures from the sanctuary, then buried it under sand. Other wells had been dug in Mecca and the Holy Well became a half-forgotten memory.

Eventually Abd al-Muttalib, a descendant of Ishmael, took on the heavy responsibility of feeding and watering all the pilgrims who came to Mecca. He dearly loved to be near the Ka'bah and sometimes slept in its close vicinity. A shadowy figure came to him on four successive nights in a vision as he slept, telling him to "Dig sweet clarity," to "Dig beneficence," to "Dig the treasured hoard," and finally to "Dig Zamzam." "What is Zamzam?" he asked. He was told to look for a place where there was blood and dung, an ants' nest and pecking ravens. He was instructed to pray "for clear flowing water that will water God's pilgrims throughout their pilgrimage."

Abd al-Muttalib found this spot in the place where people sacrificed victims to their idols, and with his son standing guard against those who objected, he began to dig with a pickaxe. Suddenly he struck the well's stone covering, and released a cry of thanksgiving to God. When he had dug out the treasure which the Jurhum had buried there, he cast lots to distribute it to the Ka'bah and to himself personally. It was also decided that his clan of Hashim would be in charge of the Well of Zamzam, since it was their responsibility to water the pilgrims.

It has been many months since Karl received this holy water. He had offered me a sip when it arrived. I took it. What was my prayer? Love. Love is my only prayer. And Karl's prayer? I have promised him I would not reveal that. But what can holy water offer but life. And what is life—truly—but love?

Reference: *Muhammad: his life based on earliest sources* by Martin Lings

New Year's Day Gifts

Five javelinas saunter past our front windows just before the sun comes up. Three adults and two young, almost full-grown. I remember seeing this family when the little ones were as big as shoeboxes. Karl and I stand to watch. A young one steps right up to the window. Its back bristles rise as it looks at me--searching, challenging, puzzled, satisfied. Its snout noses the yellow fruit of the barrel cactus, finds it not ripe to eat. It ambles off behind its family, checking here and there for breakfast. It's rare to see them in daylight. When I go for my walk a bit later, I see the neighbor's orange trash barrel knocked over, trash spilled across the road. I tell myself the javelinas found their breakfast.

I fertilize the fruit trees: orange, lemon, grapefruit, fig and pomegranate. A dry-looking pomegranate hangs from a low branch. I pluck it. The skin is cracked open, but the seeds are still moist. At lunch I share the glittering seeds with Karl. Our first pomegranate. It means something, but what is lost in time and space. Another garden, another way of marking significance. All I know is *our first pomegranate.*

I am in bed. I have just turned off the light. I lie and begin my newest ritual to quiet my mind: find three things I did today that I liked; three things I plan to do tomorrow; three things I am grateful for today; three people I want to send an extra prayer to. For some reason I open my eyes then, and see through the glass doors a meteor streak down and end in a big flash. Did I really see that? I want to see it again. In slow motion. Like on TV. I keep looking where the big flash was. I make a wish. Wait! Wishes come in threes. I make three wishes.

Finding Out

Summer of 1978 I lived in a houseful of women on Wavecrest, a walkway in Venice Beach, California. I'd lent my VW camper to Donald to drive across the country to Boston—his mother had died and he thought there might be some money left to him. I expected him back late August, early September—he'd have to enroll Pagan in school by then—but he didn't show up.

I woke up one morning with a message reverberating in my head, as if a strong voice had spoken to me: *You will know everything you need to know, when you need to know it.* As if all in capital letters. This quelled the anxiety of waiting, with no word from Donald. I had staked so much on being with him—without him I'd be lost. Rudderless.

He showed up early October with tales of woe--the camper's clutch, eating rice and beans with Pagan all across Canada—and coughing, but still smoking Camels and joints. I was so relieved to see him I didn't question that he'd already enrolled Pagan in a Santa Monica elementary school, that he'd been staying somewhere around without calling me. They stayed with me on Wavecrest until he found a two room apartment on Ozone, a walkway on the north side of Venice. His grown son, Richard, came from Boston to live with him and Pagan, so when I moved in we were four in two small rooms. Like living on a boat, I thought.

Summer of 2006 I'm happily married to Karl, living in Tucson. Kathy, Donald's third ex-wife sent me a copy of his journal, which he'd always been careful to keep private. In the five years we knew each other he'd told me many stories of his life, some of which I now saw he'd made up, like his heroics as a Marine during WWII in India. What shocked me though were the nasty things he wrote about the women in his life, including me and my young daughter.

I remembered how things went bad every which way soon after I'd moved into the Ozone apartment. Months earlier I had sent my daughter to live with her father and brother in Illinois. I thought things would be easier between Donald and me after that, but I was no longer willing to take his critical, snobbish comments. We quarreled. Donald was rude. Irascible. I put it down to his difficulty breathing. His asthma developed into emphysema. Several times I drove him to the emergency ward in the middle of the night.

He recovered some strength after a few days in the hospital over Thanksgiving 1979, and was able to drive. He and Pagan attended meetings at the Los Angeles Meher Baba Center, brought home a poster of Meher Baba, smiling, with the message: *Don't Worry, be Happy.* The only one working, I helped with finances, meals, transportation, care of Pagan, still wanting his good will. I missed my daughter. I missed my son.

On the first day of spring, 1980, Donald died.

Pagan's mother, Kathy flew in from Norfolk, Virginia the next day. She and Richard attended to all the paperwork, sorting Donald's things. Richard took his father's journals back to Boston, Kathy took Pagan back to Norfolk, I took the poster of Meher Baba and his book, *Listen Humanity*.

In my solitude Meher Baba came to me.

January to mid-March 1981, I spent in India at Baba's pilgrim center. Soon after I returned to the United States, Kathy asked me to live with them and home school Pagan. In that year, Kathy and I started a close friendship.

Twenty-five years later, Kathy sent me a copy of Donald's journal. Thanks to her, I was reading the stark thoughts of the man I had given up so much to be with. Only his sister and his daughter escaped his caustic judgments. I read with disbelief his account of a steamy affair he had with a woman in Santa Monica just before he took my camper to Boston. He took up with her again on his return, moved in with her, meaning to sever all ties with me. That fell apart on him when she demanded rent money and made it clear she didn't want Pagan around. He retaliated by dismissing her as an alcoholic and finally checking in with me.

If I had known he had deceived me in this way, would I have "taken him back"? Moved in with him and his children, borne all the discomfort of his recurring criticism? I think not. I would have left him to his proverbial devices.

But then I would not have met Kathy, now my sister-in-Baba. I would not have had the poster of Baba with its comforting message, nor have read *Listen Humanity*. And I would not have felt so bereft that Meher Baba would come to awaken my heart to His Love.

I read Donald's journal for days, assimilated my memories with his words. Echoes of old hurts. How could I have wanted to be with a man like that! Yes, he had been very good to me when we first met in Greece. So very good. That impression of a man who was kind, thoughtful, knowledgeable, intelligent, adventurous, creative and oh so cool had stayed with me for a long, long time. Still I wondered—how could I have not seen, not known... How?!

One quiet morning, in a particularly stony frame of mind, I remembered the message I'd received upon waking so many years ago: *You will know everything you need to know, when you need to know it.*

Letter Not Sent, But Shown

Dear Karl,   July 31, 2004

Being with you, I have come to know how to love these past twenty-one years. What don't you know about me? *I love you so much, you don't know*, you say. And I can hear it clear in the timbre of your voice. (I love it when you sing.) Our soul note, you call it. The steady line that weaves through the hours, the kisses and spats, the deaths and marriages, the time together and apart. My heart.

     Love always,
     Irma

Reunion - Don

I first met Don Stevens at the Fourth of July *Sahavas** at the Pilgrim Pines Retreat near Redlands, California in 1980. I use the term "met" loosely—I don't remember if I introduced myself to him or not. I remember seeing Don surrounded by Baba lovers, asking him earnest questions. I was so new to Baba that I hadn't yet formulated questions. Too shy to join the circle, I hovered at its edge.

Two or three months earlier, I'd read *Listen Humanity*, in which Don had narrated and edited the words of Meher Baba. This was the first book I'd ever read about Baba. As I read it, I had the undeniable *experience* that Meher Baba was who He said He was—the Avatar of this age, the Ancient One, God in human form. That experience was beyond faith or belief. I doubted it briefly, wondering if I'd just been alone too long and getting a tad weird. But the depth and the import of that experience never changed, never went away.

As a guest speaker, Don told us how he'd developed the habit early in his life with Baba, of reporting daily to Him, regardless of whether Baba was physically present or not. Don would talk out loud, saying whatever personal, professional and spiritual matters were presenting themselves in his life. In reporting to Baba in this manner, the issues clarified in his mind, allowing next steps and solutions to surface. He became clear on what was his to do, and what was Baba's. Perhaps these daily reports were significant in developing the depth of Don's connection with his intuition. For the past thirty years I have often followed

Don's example—reporting complex problems and situations to Baba, trusting that clarification would come.

In 2003 at my suggestion, Karl invited Don to include Tucson in his U.S. speaking tour. Don accepted and I had the privilege of picking him up at the airport. I took this ride as the opportunity to tell him about the experience I'd had while reading *Listen Humanity.*

"Ah," he said. "So you were graced with the Presence of the Avatar."

I confess that these may not have been his exact words, but they are the closest I can come to them.

His words startled me into silence. I had always known that my experience had been extraordinary, but I'd never thought that I'd actually had Meher Baba's *darshan.***

For two days Don spoke at meetings at our home. We had a full house—the largest gathering of Baba lovers I'd ever seen in Tucson. Later, Nancy Wall, Karl and I co-wrote an article about this event for the London (Don's home at the time) Meher Baba newsletter.

In May 2010, Karl and I received email announcements of the 2010 Beads on One String Tour—a chance to visit several sacred sites in India with Don and other Baba lovers from around the world. We both recognized this as the chance of a lifetime, and quickly agreed to send in our applications. On the phone with our daughter, Stephanie, I told her about our exciting plans.

"I saw that email too," she said. "I thought to myself, Mom and Karl should go on that tour. And then she said, "If you go, I'll pay for the tour part."

Thank you, sweet daughter! Thank you, Baba!

Karl and I arrived in New Delhi two days before the tour started so we could begin to get over the jet lag. We saw Don in the hotel restaurant and said our hellos. 'Irene' he called me. I bent close to his ear and said softly, "My name is Irma." He smiled and nodded.

Don was ninety-two by this time—doing well except for his knees, which were fragile. Throughout the trip he got around with the help of a cane, a wheelchair or sometimes strong arms supporting him on both sides. But in no other way was he fragile—at our first tour group meeting Don was in complete charge, brooking no nonsense, as they say.

A few days later at Mt. Abu, home of the Jain Temples, he called me 'Irene' again. I didn't say anything this time. It didn't seem to matter. A day or two later, we'd travelled far south on an overnight train to Mahabaleshwar, a hill station covered with cloud.

Fatigue and a touch of intestinal ailment kept me and a few others from joining the group to visit Arthur's Seat, an overlook made famous among Baba lovers because of a glorious photo of Meher Baba standing there. I made a sincere effort to let go of my deep disappointment. The following morning some of us did not feel up to climbing 562 steps to see Shivaji's Fort. But we did feel well enough to take a cab, then manage the dozen or two steps down to Arthur's Seat, shrouded in cloud.

Later I was sitting near Don on the coach (tour bus). He leaned over and asked, "How did you find Arthur's Seat?"

"Mystical," I said. Purely mist-ical."

He smiled and nodded. "Can you forgive me for calling you 'Irene' again?"

I was most surprised that he'd realized he'd done that. "I'll take it into consideration," I said with just enough mock archness that he nodded and smiled.

Two days later we were in Hyderabad, staying at the Jubilee Hills Meher Baba Retreat. I approached Don just before breakfast in the dining room, and said, "In 1948 we boarded a ship in Bremershafen, emigrating to Canada. The first song I ever heard in English was 'Goodnight Irene.' So maybe you were on to something." He nodded and smiled.

Later that day, Don announced he was having an interview videotaped after we had chanted and meditated in the Manonash Cave, where Meher Baba had ended the New Life. He wanted to record the impressions and experiences of the tour, and had chosen a few tour members to be interviewed.

"If anyone has any questions or issues with whom I have chosen, I want to hear them." He named some of those who had been on the Beads 2009 tour, so they could compare and contrast their experiences of the two trips. Then he said, "And I also want to include Irma and Karl."

Once again his words startled me into silence. Why me? My mind scurried looking for plausible reasons—it came up with several, but none good enough to latch on to. I realized that unless I asked him, I would never know. And I knew I would never ask him. It would have to remain a mystical thing.

Some of the Beads (tour group members) have kept in touch via email. After I sent a comment on something, Don wrote he was happy to hear from me, and welcomed my continued contributions. This set my head spinning again. Was he this solicitous with everyone? I remembered looking into his eyes, seeing profound warmth, kindness and acceptance. Why did this always surprise me so? As if I expected distance or dismissal from a male authority figure. Another mystery.

Just before Christmas, I sent a photo of myself riding Calvin, the camel, along with my Camel poem to all the Beads, including Don. This brought me another sweet note from Don. Even though he was recuperating in France from surgery on a broken leg, he was busy planning the 2011 Beads tour.

In retrospect I am aware of a sense of healing in my heart, connected with all my interactions with Don. Throughout the Beads tour, I felt the warmth of having been admitted, accepted, even chosen.

January 18, 2011 Addendum: In response to an email from Karl encouraging Don to get stronger soon so he could head up the

European Beads Tour, Don wrote back that he would be on the Med (Mediterranean) Basin bonanza "...and I look forward to being with you and Irma or *else*."

I'm beginning to think of Don as my dear and long-lost uncle.

* *sahavas* - a gathering held by the Master so that his devotees may enjoy his company
** *darshan*– the appearance or audience of the Master on some occasion, to bestow blessings on devotees

Reunion -Home

Karl and I flew from Tucson to Chicago, then over the northern tip of Greenland to the northern coast of Russia. Our travel agent told us we would fly over the North Pole. We flew close to, but not over it, and a young part of me was disappointed—I'd so looked forward to telling people, *...and we flew over the North Pole!* We flew over Russia, Afghanistan, Pakistan and on to New Delhi, India. After that our travels were by train and hired coaches: a train to Ajmer, a coach to Mt. Abu, an overnight train (first class) to Mahabaleshwar, a coach to Satara, then Pune, overnight trains (third class) to Hyderabad and (first class) to Aurangabad, a coach to Valley of the Saints near Khuldabad, a coach to the Ellora Caves, and finally to Meherabad.

Welcome Home.

In each place we had stayed one or two nights in excellent hotels and once in a pilgrim hostel. In each place we had to identify and learn how to navigate the way to our rooms, the lighting, heating, cooling systems, how to flush the toilets, how the hot and cold water and bathing facilities were arranged, and how to find the dining rooms. We had to be sure to have enough bottled water to drink and to brush our teeth with through each day and night. The tour guides were exemplary in providing large bottles of water to everyone on each leg of train and coach travel. Each morning we had to figure out what was best to wear—in steamy green cultivated fields, in chilly, clouded hill stations, on the overnight trains. En route we had to negotiate public toilets and washrooms, some with Western-style sit down toilets, some with Indian squatting facilities.

Perhaps we were kept so busy with these minutiae to keep us out of trouble. Of course, almost each one of us had a brush or two with intestinal, and sometimes respiratory ailments, despite all precautions. For almost three weeks we were in perpetual motion, with brief stops in new places, and then—Home!

Not home in Tucson.

Nana Kher, one of Meher Baba's mandali, used to welcome pilgrims to Baba's *Samadhi*,* giving each one an embrace and saying, *Welcome Home*. I remember the first time he said that to me. I had a vague idea of what he meant, but my heart was still guarded. It didn't *feel* like home. What I know now is that I was not yet at home within myself. I wasn't there yet. Nana Kher is gone now, perhaps to his eternal Home, and I often remember his gentle ways.

When our coach entered Ahmednagar, an old and dusty ramble of an Indian city, five miles from Meherabad, my senses perked up. I know this place. I've been here many times before. The coach rumbled down the road to Meherabad, the road now filled with trucks, taxis, private cars, motorcycles, rickshaws and bicycles, and dotted with cows, bullock carts, dogs, goats and pedestrians with jars or bundles atop their heads. Just like in all the other Indian cities. New houses, new businesses had sprung up along the roadside since our last visits in 2002 and 2007. Gone were many of the fields of millet. My eyes noted the changes. My mind noted that I *knew* there were changes.

At last the coach turned left into Lower Meherabad and came to a stop in front of the Meher Pilgrim Centre. We climbed down and entered the dear, old MPC, where I'd stayed many times in the past thirty years. My footsteps light and winging—I knew this place. I'd slept in this room, and this and this. I ate in this dining hall, played Scrabble and chatted long hours here with other pilgrims. I knew where the bathrooms were—I remembered being very sick in this one. The gardens were still alive with birds, the porticos continued to give shelter from sun, and the long verandas always invited solitude or companionable chats.

Pat and Irene greeted us—so sweet to see them— I've known them for decades. They helped us fill out registration forms, and then we boarded the coach one last time. It took us to the new MPR, a sprawling elegance of simplicity and light. *I know this place too,* my heart sang. *I've been here before.* I'd asked for and was given a private room. After weeks of being packed in and herded about with twenty-five lovely pilgrims, I figured I'd want a bit of solitude.

Welcome Home!

It wasn't just that I knew many of the residents, and where our rooms were, how the bathrooms and toilets worked, that the reading rooms stayed open all day and night, that I knew where to take my laundry and where to take the path to Baba's *Samadhi*. It was that *I knew and felt in all parts of myself, inside and out, that I was Home.* I was finally *here*.

* *Samadhi* - Meher Baba's Tomb, a place of worship.

These Are the Good Old Days
After reading the book and seeing the movie, "The Road."

Not perfect, but we have food, water, air. We have a sound and beautiful home. We have clothes, cars, furnishings, dishes, pots, pans, flatware and sharp knives. We have a washer, dryer, stove, refrigerator, freezer, dishwasher, toaster oven, grill and food processor. We have all the food we need, including chocolate. We have television, radio, videos, CDs, DVDs, cameras, field glasses, cell phones, land lines, computers, printers, scanners and fax machines. We have a piano, digital pianos, didgeridoos, harmonicas, drums, bells and rainsticks.

We have mesquite, palo verde, orange, lemon, grapefruit, pomegranate and fig trees, and a grapevine. Shrubbery and flowers—roses, bougainvillea, nandini, petunias, desert marigold, hackberry, brittlebush and lilies. I won't mention all the cacti. We have glorious mountains, endless blue skies, sunshine and some rain.

We have bobcats, coyotes, javelinas, raccoons, rattlesnakes, other snakes, tarantulas, hawks, owls, woodpeckers, bats, bees, butterflies, dragonflies, moths and a few mosquitoes. We have rosy dawns, high noons and fiery sunsets. We have spangled night sky parades featuring Orion, the Big Dipper, Cassiopeia, the Pleiades, Gemini, Scorpio and the moon full, smiling or shy by turn. We don't have earthquakes, floods, tsunamis, hurricanes, tornadoes or volcanoes.

We have cats--brother and sister. We have a loving daughter and son-in-law. We have friends to play and dance with. We have friends to pray and sing with. We have love and work that challenges and sustains us. These *are* the good old days.

Going Home

There is no home to go back to. Not just because my parents have long been dead. Not just because we lived in the house my father built in Windsor, Canada for only eight years, or even because of the sad, bad things that happened there. Perhaps a bit because the row house we rented on Lillian Street for five years has been torn down. The rooms we rented on first coming to Windsor were no homes, just temporary refuges. Toeholds as immigrants. Nor Uncle John's farm in Saskatchewan, which we inhabited like ghosts that first winter. Certainly not the immigration camps in Germany. I did go back, after fifteen years, to the Bavarian village of my first memories, where we lived in Frau Heilmeier's farm parlor, all four of us, after the war. Spent an afternoon there--nothing there for me except that the villagers remembered my family by name. And not the city where I was born in Silesia, whose name has either been so drastically changed into Polish that it's unrecognizable, or it was blasted to bits in the spring of 1945. I never find it on the maps. Nor have I kept my father's name. Home is here now. It abides within me, through all changes.

The Bemused Smile

The look on the clerk's face was a cross between bemused and quizzical. Was there something odd about asking for fifteen dollars worth of gas?

"Fifteen--one five?" he repeated.

"Fifteen." I nodded and set the bills on the counter.

I was on my way to Rick's Import Service for my Element's regular service appointment. When I'd started the car this morning I saw the gas was so low that the warning light was on. Running out of gas is on my lifelong list of extremely tedious things to do. I planned to stop at the Chevron station on the way, where I could use my card.

But as I approached it, I was surprised to see it was no longer a Chevron station, so I drove on, hoping to find another on the way. No luck. Desperate, I pulled into a Food Mart. I had to pay cash there, so I went inside.

After the clerk punched in my fifteen dollars of gas at pump number four--which occasioned another bemused smile when I said I didn't know which pump I was at--I turned to leave.

Then it hit me! I had spoken!

It was Silence Day, July 10th.

No wonder the clerk looked at me oddly. I had a colorful sign hanging from my neck: "I am observing silence today."

And here at seven-twenty in the morning I had already broken my silence. In thirty-three years I have never been successful in maintaining silence on this day. Each year I feel tricked into a bit of mundane speech. I have heard that Meher Baba's sister, Mani, also was never successful in maintaining one hundred per cent silence on Silence Day. Whether it's true or not, this story gives me comfort.

Shaking my head at myself, I pumped gas into the Element, and remembered the coyote that crossed the road in front of me as I left home this morning. Unusual to see them in broad daylight. I knew it meant something. Coyote, the Trickster!

I wanted to be an archeologist when I was twelve

but now,
unlike some bit of winter blasting
down from Saskatoon,
I sweep gently at the dust covering
my true self,
blow lightly at family dirtstorms,
screen their troubling debris,
brush off their ancient insults,
tap tenderly at layers of ancestral beliefs,
peel away the stubborn layers of self-interest
plastered on my psyche,
and slowly, slowly
uncover the bonebits, the sinews and casings
that hold my heart secure
despite ravages of hoar and heat,
of loss, of hurt, of time.

Scaffolding

Wanting takes me to do this, get that. It does its job by providing a scaffold for His work.

Karl and I are refinancing our house. A fifteen year mortgage at a lower interest rate, the same monthly payment. Six years and fifty-three thousand dollars off our current loan agreement. Instead of working till I'm ninety, I only have to walk down the hall into my office until I'm eighty-four. This sounds more reasonable, possibly even doable.

I see myself, finally with solid grey hair--in my Herman Miller swivel chair, listening to the same stories of dysfunctional family life, leading to the same unhappy relationships between husbands and wives, between fathers, sons, mothers, daughters, friends and coworkers. What will keep me going?

The view of prickly pear and palo verde outside the door. Cottontail bunnies looking for mesquite beans. Lizards doing push-ups, scooting over the doormat. The calls of the Pyrrhuloxia, the white-winged dove, the woodpecker. The occasional bobcat strolling past the window. A road runner racing across the drive. The honeyed scent of mimosa, the pungency of chaparral. The dance of pine branches by the window. Wind soughing in the eaves. An ocean of clouds in blue sky. The promise of rain.

Who knows how long I will last? How long I need the scaffolding of this body to swivel in this chair. It is my heart that He is building strong and true.

Love's Journey

I barely loved my first husband. It took us seven years to figure that out. I can't say whether he ever loved me or not. It didn't feel like it. We'd say, "I love you," as if to make it come true.

After years of spirited single life, I met Donald on a park bench in Greece. We camped all summer around the Peloponnus, smoking hash every night, diving deep into sexual pleasure, telling our stories afterward. One night I said, "I can love you, Donald." Despite being stoned, I knew I meant it.

Eventually through him, I came to know of Meher Baba, who said, "True love is not for the faint of heart." That proved to be true in the harsh realities of my life with Donald, all the way to his death five years after we met. My love true enough to bring me home to Meher Baba.

I can't write about love. It's too much like the five blind men grasping at different parts of the elephant. Meher Baba said, "Things that are Real are given and received in silence."

Karl and I have been married for thirty-one years now. I have grown to love him deeply, truly. In part, that means I have come to accept him as he is, and my capacity for self-acceptance has deepened to an equal degree.

Morning Walk

My shadow stretches out before me,
confident, grander than life.
I want it to walk beside me—
no room, it says, the path is too narrow.
It's true—prickly pear, barrel cactus, cholla loom
from each side of the stony way.
I clamber down, watch out
for loose rocks and snakes.
My shadow lengthens,
joggles around, seems to laugh
as if leading me along, showing the way.
It longs for tea with cream,
slender hips, wash and wear hair,
pelicans skirting the seashore,
breathing easy under fluorescent skies.
This is the life, it says—like this.
I lean in to hear better—
suddenly
feel a stone in my shoe,
a thorn in my sock.
By the time I've emptied my shoe,
my shadow, less jaunty,
has emptied itself, curling
up into me as if for refuge,
as if for dreamless sleep,
leaving me awakened.

A cardinal flames before me.

Game Complete

My passing seems like a coming attraction.
Let it be quick—I will be ready, all unpacked—
my every mental impression spent, all forgiven.

Like a game of solitaire—the cards aligned,
matched up—game complete. No ambitions,
desires, fears, tirades, no longings left

hanging—even tea with cream on a rainy
afternoon, sleeping cats curled into their tails.
Husband, child, friend I will love forever.

I'll have let go of the newest moon, Orion
and his flashy companions. Adieu petunia's
fuchsia trumpet, honeysuckle evenings,

coyotes' electric concerts. O, to pass over
that invisible threshold. Not one care
for epitaph or gravestone to mark where

I am not. Ashes into the wind. Spirit free
to migrate through Love's open door,
merge into the Sun of suns, drown

in everlasting lasting bliss.

my legacy

trail of sandalwood
from an empty chair--
echoes of humming
dancing in the kitchen

Christmas is crowded

                        all full of stuff
of things made in China there's never enough
walls, tables, closets and shelves
piled with Santas, reindeer and elves
yards, cars, rooftops seen to carry
blown-up snowmen, Jesus, Joseph and Mary
trees made in China with ornaments to boot
bells, balls and birds, whimsical and cute
mistletoe and wreaths of red, green and gold
decorate doorways, bright, berried and bold
stockings hang empty, wait by the fires
to be hopefully filled with little desires
while Frosty and Rudolf waltz in delight
winking 'n blinking *Merry Christmas*
                      all through the night.

Mind/Body

In September 2011, Karl and I planned to fly to Seattle to visit our daughter. A few days before our flight I lost one of my hearing aids in my home office. It was just suddenly gone! I looked everywhere in my office. Fifteen hundred dollars to replace it! Frantic, I looked again and again. Every surface, every drawer, behind and under the desk, carpet, sofa, chairs. I kept "suddenly seeing it." Part of me knew it would suddenly appear, so I searched obsessively for two days.

To no avail. But it dawned on me that my body was not upset-- no stomach tension, no neck , shoulder or headaches. I believe the body is the truth-teller, whereas the mind can make up all kinds of stories. I decided to trust my body. We packed. We flew. I forgot about my hearing aid while we were in Seattle.

A few days after our return, I was with a client in my office. I pulled out a large reference book to share some information. On its open pages I saw--suddenly--my hearing aid! I remembered then that I'd consulted this same book the day the hearing aid had disappeared. It must have slipped out of my ear and fallen onto the open book without my noticing it.

Most interesting to me was that once I was aware that my body was not disturbed, my mind also calmed itself, and I was able to enjoy our trip to Seattle without worry.

The Telephone Call --2012

On the evening of February 14th, Valentine's Day, I made a fire in our fireplace. I set up tray tables in the study, facing the beehive fireplace. Karl put Bach's Brandenburg Concerto on. We had steak, roasted potatoes and salad. Chocolate cake for dessert. Minnie and Max sat patiently for bites of steak, then sprawled on the rug near our feet, soaking up the warmth. Having dinner in front of the fire was a treat for us, the few times we did each winter.

When the phone rang, I answered, being closest to it.

"Hi Mom!" It was Stephanie.

"Where are you--in India?"

"Yeah, just outside the dining hall."

It was unusual for her to call from India. In fact, she had never done that before, since emails worked so well for whatever communications were necessary.

"Are you alright?"

I knew she'd gone to Meher Baba's Pilgrim Retreat a couple of weeks earlier to meet up with Ahmad, the young man from Shiraz. He'd been asking her to marry him for two years now.

"I'm calling because I have something to tell you, Mom. Ahmad and I are engaged. He asked me again, and I said yes this time."

"Congratulations. That's wonderful news on Valentine's Day, Stephanie. I hope you and Ahmad will be very happy."

"It's not Valentine's Day here now. It's morning already. We went to the bazaar and he bought me two rings, because here you're supposed to have three rings--I made a third one out of my hair thingie. Then we went to Bhau, who blessed us."

I pictured the scenes as she spoke. Saw her sitting in the office across from the dining hall at the Meher Pilgrim Retreat. Ahmad watching her face.

"That's good, to get Bhau's blessing."

"Ahmad is here. He wants to say something to you."

"Okay." She put Ahmad on the phone.

"Hello, my Mother!" he said. Loud, exuberant, sweet.

"Hello, Ahmad. Jai Meher Baba!"

Stephanie came back on the line, saying they would apply for a fiance visa, for him to come to the United States.

What were the chances of the United States Immigration officials permitting a young man from a Moslem family in Shiraz, Iran, to enter in these times?

But we all knew in Whose Hands that decision really rested.

Where's Max?

The day after Christmas, a young bobcat suddenly appeared at the dining room window in front of me as I ate breakfast. I sat quietly, watched it peer inside, then move around the firecracker bush to the south gate. I rose to follow its path. It stood peering through the gate, till suddenly its head recoiled, and after another hard look, it backed up and paced quickly around Karl's studio and disappeared. I wondered what could have startled it so. Surely not Max.

A moment later Max, our black cat, came in. As I finished breakfast he scurried about, slung low to the floor, as if feeling anxious, threatened. By what, I wondered. The bobcat was out front, not at all in the backyard. I washed and dressed, getting ready for my ten o'clock client. I didn't see Max in his usual morning places, so I looked in all his places--even outside, though it was too cool for him to hang out there now. I didn't see him anywhere. Could there be a bobcat in the backyard? I looked through all the windows, but saw no movement. Maybe Max was hiding in the house after seeing the bobcat through the gate.

After my client left, I searched again for Max--in closets, under our bed, behind the sofa and other unlikely places. Out front I called his name, though he wouldn't have had a way to get out there. I stepped into the backyard and called *Max!* and clapped my hands, our old signal for him to come running. This wasn't the first time he'd seemed to have disappeared.

Instead, something streaked out of the Texas Ranger hedge and into the cat yard. Something that was not black. I walked to the entrance of the cat yard and saw a hefty bobcat jumping up repeatedly, trying in vain to get over our eight-foot fence, with a T-section across the top. I unlocked the north gate, left it open for him to find his way out. I waited by the house for a few minutes until he did, then locked the gate again. This was a different bobcat from the one I saw out front.

I was afraid of what I already knew I would find in the corner under the hedge. Max, lying still, his leg torn. I said his name. He didn't move. A fly buzzed around his head.

I returned to this spot with a heavy plastic bag, forced my way through a thicket of Texas Ranger branches. Max's body was still warm, soft. Gently I picked it up, slid it into the bag and backed out of the hedge. I set the bag down next to the house. Looked carefully at Max, where he'd been ravaged. I looked particularly at his face, still his dear, sweet face. How many times he had gazed at me with love and trust. I stroked his head. And cried. Since Max had felt nervous, he probably saw the bobcat in the backyard. *Why* did he go outside?

I tucked the bag closed to keep insects out. E-mailed Karl at work: something has happened to Max. Call me if you can. Karl called after two o'clock. I told him a bobcat had gotten Max. I could hear the tears in his voice, *Oh no! I'll come home now.*

We dug a hole as deeply as we could in a corner of the cat yard. I spread Max's soft blanket, brown with beige paw prints all over, at the bottom of the hole. Laid Max on it. I carried Minnie, who has lost her sight, from her safe place on the loveseat to Max's grave. Set her down to let her sniff him. She immediately growled and hissed and struggled to get away. What did she smell--Max's body or the bobcat's scent on him? I picked her up and brought her back to her safe place.

Karl and I said Meher Baba's prayers--O Parvardigar, the Prayer of Repentance and Beloved God, tears intervening with each of us. I stroked Max's out-stretched paw. Covered him with his blanket. We took handfuls of earth to spread over Max's covered form. Then shovelfuls, until there was a small mound. Gathered large, heavy stones from the cat yard to place on the mound.

We went inside and had tea. We cried. Suddenly I saw the bobcat leap up onto the pine tree in front of the house and jump onto our roof. We ran to the backyard. Karl threw handfuls of gravel up onto the roof. No sign of the bobcat. We went out front--no sign there either.

It's hard to say if Minnie misses Max. She's so disoriented already due to her loss of sight. She must, though. They'd been together for eighteen years.

The next day I saw Max in all his usual places at all the usual times, and missed him. I felt disoriented. It was hard to look at the hedge. I sent an e-mail to friends who knew Max, telling briefly what had happened and our sadness. I printed a photo I'd taken of him last summer. Framed it and put it on the kitchen counter. Every time I looked at it, I saw him. His spirit must still have been with us.

I saw those two bobcats twice in the past few days. Once on the road in front of our house, and again walking all along the driveway in front of our house. One much bigger than the other--a mom and her half-grown cub?

Yesterday I felt a shift. The tears subsiding. I have taken in, absorbed his absence. I feel he has moved on too. Years ago someone told us Max was very disappointed he wasn't a dog in this lifetime. Next life--a sweet puppy? Vesta e-mailed that she prayed he would be born into a loving Baba family.

Minnie -- August 14, 1996 - January 19, 2014

Minnie lies beside me on the loveseat,
curled comfy on her soft rug.
Her paws, ears and whiskers twitch--
she is dreaming.
In her dreams she can still see,
go after the moth, the bird, the rat.

Awake, eyes open
she can't see me watching her--
stretches so slowly.

Minnie moves carefully,
one measured limb at a time,
as if checking its ability
before trusting her weight on it.

She sleeps again.
I want to kiss her black nose.
I hold her snow-white feet.

Cats over Dogs

A walk in the desert beats a Sunday in church.
Tea beats coffee and cream, not milk.
Toni Childs hands down over Barbra Streisand.
Clouds to punctuate sky rather than endless blue.
Dark chocolate over milk duds.
Live plants and flowers over paper, plastic, even silk.
Cheap thrills, never horror chills--
Space Mountain, not Stephen King.
Ravens and crows over blackbirds or starlings.
Gold over silver.
Scrabble over Trivial Pursuit.
A day at the beach over any casino.
Cartoons over editorials.
Fast dance over slow.
A book of my own and leisure on a quiet bench
outdoes a borrowed one in a library's dry confines.
A rose rather than an orchid.
A tall tale over a shifty story.
Mountains over plains.
Blues and greens over reds and yellows.
To see and be seen with eyes of kindness
rather than any look of appraisal or desire.

Balance,
but the bottom line must always be heart over head.

Some Poems

like so many empty boxes
after the Christmas tree spree,
litter my books.

A few still hold heat,
something given and taken
heart to heart.

No Resistance

Love like water
flows
into spaces of least resistance.

God as Love
resides
in places of least resistance.

When I least resist
God,
I am deeply fulfilled.

When I have no resistance
to Love,
I will be one with God.

Irma Sheppard was born Irmhild Hexel in Germany in 1943. Her family emigrated to Canada in 1948 and to the United States in 1962. She has lived in Michigan, California, Virginia, and for the past thirty-some years with her husband and a succession of cats in Tucson, Arizona, where she is in private practice as a psychotherapist. Her short story, "The Human Touch: A Triptych" won the Martindale Literary Award in 2000, and was published in *Kaleidoscope*, an anthology of Martindale winners. Her short story, "A Real Piece of India" was published in *SandScript* and in *Portrait.* She edited and co-*authored Beads On One String Tour 2010* and *Beads-on-One-String Heartland Pilgrimage 2013*. Her first book of poems, *Inheritance,* came out in 2013.

ihs222@theriver.com

www.ingramcontent.com/pod-product-compliance
Lightning Source LLC
Chambersburg PA
CBHW051937290426
44110CB00015B/2018